10 COMMANDMENTS FOR DREAM CHASERS

DREAM LIKE GOD IS CHEERING FOR YOU

Kimberley M. Byrd

Word Eternal
PUBLISHING

Copyright ©2018 by Kimberley M. Byrd
All rights reserved.

Published by Word Eternal Publishing, Inc.
P.O. Box 625, Troy, AL 36081

Printed in the United States of America

Library of Congress Cataloging-in-Publication Data

ISBN 10: 0-9794433-3-4
ISBN 13: 978-0-9794433-3-6

For speaking engagements, please contact the author at:

Kimberley M. Byrd
www.WriteOnKim.com

Scripture taken from the New King James Version®. Copyright © 1982 by Thomas Nelson, Inc. Used by permission. All rights reserved.

Scripture taken from the Holy Bible King James Version, copyright © 2006 by Hendrickson Publishers, Peabody, Massachusetts. Used by permission. All rights reserved.

Scripture quotations marked (AMP) are taken from the Amplified Bible, Copyright © 1954, 1958, 1962, 1964, 1965, 1987 by The Lockman Foundation. Used by permission.

Cover Photo: Theaucitron

This book is dedicated to the Best-Selling Author of all time, the Giver of every dream. And to my parents, Albert and Pastelene McClure, who are now eternally in His presence.

In addition, I dedicate this book to you, the stubborn dreamer who is in search for one more word of confirmation to make the final decision that you were not born to quit.

Contents

Foreword	7
Introduction	9
I. Don't F.E.A.R.	15
II. Daily Bread	29
III. Declare It	42
IV. Dangle the Dream Before You	51
V. Delete & Defeat Your Demons	57
VI. Don't Tell It; Live It	64
VII. Dream Protection	71
VIII. Decoding the Detours	83
IX. Develop Positive Connections	92
X. Die Empty	106
Final Word	111
Acknowledgments	115
About the Author	117

Foreword

A few weeks before the release of this book, I had a dream that I asked the author to let me see this book. In my dream, she went to the fellowship hall and came back handing it to me. The following Sunday from the pulpit, I told her that it was time to release this book and that someone needed it. After service, she informed me she had just asked God a week before in a quick inward prayer to let her know when to release this particular work, which was already completed but tucked away inside of her computer.

This book, Ten Commandments for Dream Chasers: Dream Like God is Cheering for You, contains information that can help you achieve your dreams and become a successful Dream Conqueror. The author, Kimberley M. Byrd discusses 10 commandments or principles that will help usher your dreams into reality. As you journey through the pages, read at a pace of understanding, asking yourself one question, what do I really want from my dreams?

The information that is before you is only for encouragement, not to work your dream. Dreams are somewhat like our children. We birth them, care for them, and then we expect something in return. Why spend time dreaming when you are not willing to invest in your dreams? Working for your dream now will bring you benefits later. If you believe in your dreams and are not working for your dreams, your dreams will not survive. The bible talks about faith without works is dead and works without faith is dead. When faith and works are combined, they become the right team for a successful and moving dream that will bring you a prosperous life. Remember your dreams are bigger than you think. Joseph's dreams were not just for him or his people but his dreams included the whole world because it was God's plan. Don't let your dreams end up in a garbage bag at a Dream Chaser abortion clinic. Be careful who you share your dream with. Don't let negative people speak over your dreams. Their words will breed fear and doubt into the heart of your dream. Know who you are connecting with; family members will love you but dishonor your dreams; friends can appreciate you but hate your dreams. Live your dreams everyday by declaring them unto the Lord who is the giver of all dreams. Keep your relationship open with Him through prayer.

    The author, Kimberley M. Byrd is a minister at Cornerstone of Life Church where I pastor. One Sunday while she was ministering, she said, "I won't be here much longer." From that message God powerfully birthed in her The Ten Commandments for Dream Chasers. Since that Sunday, I have noticed her confidence shifting into higher dimensions as she is functioning with more assertion of I can do it. I have personally watched Kimberley experience and struggle with many heartbreaking dreams in the past, but today I can truly say her life testifies and defines the characteristics of a Dream Chaser!

—Pastor James McClure
Cornerstone of Life

Introduction

So you want to pursue your dream? Why? An even greater question is why now? Answering these questions will help in the process when the heat intensifies to the point you question your decision. Why? Has the desire been burning inside to start or complete something; something you have been ignoring or at least attempting to for a while? Why now? Are the feelings of urgency pressing you creating a very distressing experience knocking you from your comfort zone? The flame is being kindled inside of you at this particular time for a purpose greater than you, a season without distinction, and possibly, for an individual or individuals you have never met. At this point, all there is are mental images of a hopeful future success. It's the in between which will bring you to your knees wondering what you have gotten yourself into contemplating quitting.

However, on the flip side, the side you are on now is not any better. You've been stagnant long enough sulking in the despair of learning that quitting and not even trying are one in the same. Internally, you know there will not be any peace until you seek it out or pursue it. There is a still small voice saying to you that this is the time to do it. What is "it"? Yet another question you will have to answer. You are probably thinking to yourself that thus far this book is somewhat discouraging. Maybe you were thinking it would be filled with colorful quotes of motivation but let me make one statement which will jar you into believing and knowing this is one of the best books you will ever read when it comes to getting you closer to where you need to be. Here it is: no soldier goes to the spa to be pampered before combat. Dream chasing is a battle. I have the scars to prove it. And if I am going to be a God writer then I am going to come at you with a combatant style of truth you may not like but you will definitely thank me later.

Every gift is from God, the Creator of everything. As long as you are sitting still, not doing anything but wasting the gift God has placed on the inside of you, no one has a problem with you except for your inner self who knows you are purposed for a more productive life. The very moment you decide to live, to dream, to finish, trouble swarms you. It is almost as if once you recognize the force on the inside, opposition becomes attracted to you. Why? It is all to make you quit; to not walk in the power God Almighty has given you.

Peter writes, "God has given each of you a gift from his great variety of spiritual gifts. Use them well to serve one another…Do it with all the strength and energy that God supplies. Then everything you do will bring glory to God through Jesus Christ."

When you go after those desires, goals, visions, or dreams, that press you from within, you are only acting out your innate ability to chase, to conquer, to win. Don't quit. It is supposed to get hard. If it were easy your appreciation level would not be high enough to give Him glory. Your uncommon feat will be minimized into "anyone can do that." If the wonderful Creator of everything endorses you, then nothing else matters. But here is a caveat; if your mind does not link up with what He wants to do through you to place on the earth to be an inheritance, a

INTRODUCTION

possession for His people, then you will never run the lap of victory. You have to make a decision. Make it now.

To be a Dream Chaser is to become a person with a multilevel thought process who yields herself to the service of the Lord. Yielding takes trust, surrendering, and humility; the mind to relinquish the control of something highly precious to you. When accustomed to doing things on your own, so you thought, this is a hard lesson to learn. Here is the place where you need to revisit Jeremiah 29:11 often. It will remind you that God is not trying to hurt you but wants so much more from you even while you are in a place of bondage; He can still prosper you.

The day before I completed this book, 10 Commandments for Dream Chasers, the subtitle revealed itself to me after months of being in search of it. Dream like God is cheering for you was the encouragement I needed to finish and finish well. Then although I thought I was finished another three years would pass before I got the approval to revisit with the intent to complete the assignment. Those three hellacious years proved that the same motivation I desired to give to others could be shattered within my soul. During this time period, I was tested in the very areas I was writing on. Now, I write from a realm of credibility given to me by experience.

Therefore, most of the hard lessons in here are close to my heart since they had to be personally lived before written. God is very particular about what His people consume and His writers must listen carefully; judgment is inevitable.

We can learn lessons from His word about how to handle opposition well without quitting or acting out of character. He had many writers that listened, writing the story of themselves and others to get the point across that God is Sovereign and unstoppable. If He says it is going to happen, it is. You might cry, but do not give up or give in. The Almighty One is on your side.

In the bible, many extraordinary people accomplished uncommon acts only by the strength of God placed within them. In your reading of this book, you may read references to Joseph, the dreamer, since he is a testament of how to have a dream, go through whatever it takes, stay the course, and live the dream. It is necessary to see what it looks like to have opposition coming from within the family unit, those who are closest to you. God is unstoppable.

Then David will be referenced to give a visual of how to have a gift growing on the inside of you that gets you in trouble even before the personal recognition of what is there is even made. He projects the image of what it is like to be laughed at and discredited because you do not look the part of neither king nor giant slayer. Regardless of the circumstances or mistakes, he is esteemed a man after God's heart. God is unstoppable.

Abraham, the father of faith, shows us how to believe without an immediate reason to; crazy faith in the face of circumstances which could very possibly cause doubt. His faith exemplifies doing exactly what God says even to inches of taking the life of the promise. The father of faith shows us what it is like to walk in obedience regardless of the lack of knowledge of the ram in the bush.

There are examples from the Bible, but there are many principles that came from the wisdom given to one who writes for Him. If properly received and used, you will set yourself on a course that will change the rest of your life.

A hesitance came with using the term Dream Chaser; actually, I kept noticing people come against the term relating it to those who do not finish but just keep running behind the dream. That fact alone is what made me choose to keep it; we are always chasing after or in pursuit of God and will do so until our life is no more.

INTRODUCTION

With continual chasing, it means our life does not belong to us nor is our dream singular. Remember what Peter wrote; God has *many* gifts that He releases to His people. His receiving glory is continual. God is unstoppable. With you being created in His image, so are you. Dream to the best of your ability for God is cheering for you.

So many of our dreams at first seem impossible, then they seem improbable, and then, when we summon the will, they soon become inevitable.—Christopher Reeves

I. Don't F.E.A.R.

Your heart is pounding hard in your chest; breathing irregular. The finish line is ahead; the cheers of the crowd crescendo the closer you get. Now they are in sight with a familiar silhouette coming into view. It is someone who you know is cheering for you. You see their fists pumping violently in the air as they jump up and down. Knowing someone is on your side, cheering for you, you dig deeper ignoring the weariness of your body. A second wind has hit you as you make a mad dash to completion.

Merely knowing someone is in your corner gives you a boost of adrenaline pushing you to perform better dismissing the willingness to quit. This level of external encouragement helps in receiving the victory if we just do not fear.

At this point, have you really absorbed the subtitle of this book? Has it been applied to the transformation process of your mindset? The affect shows up when you develop the attitudes of quitting is not an option and victory is around the corner. When you go after your dreams like God is the one at the finish line, if you know God, your faith increases to an optimal level in which you truly do not have the capacity to understand. Your decision-making process changes. If its meaning has not been engrafted into your heart yet then you are still susceptible to F.E.A.R.

To define fear would be to say it is one of those emotions, once it gets a hand on you, grips so tightly it will suffocate you from trying. The dictionary says fear is a distressing emotion aroused by impending danger, evil, pain, etc., whether the threat is real or imagined; the feeling or condition of being afraid. What are you afraid of?

My definition of F.E.A.R. is Foolish Examination About Reality. Reality is that God is bigger than anything you can ever face yet we cringe when the right level of opposition comes in. Per the dictionary's definition, we can get spooked just from thinking something is going to happen to us. Nothing has materialized and we put on the brakes. We have foolishly given the power over.

Don't Drown

I have a personal experience with almost meeting my demise in the Atlantic Ocean bordering Miami, Florida. After spending a long time playing a great distance from the shore yet in waist deep water, I decided to go back onto the beach to rest. While walking back, I became submerged into a deeper area as the ground was uneven in several places. That was not the problem. The point where the problem entered was that I became entangled in fishing wire although at the time this was unknown to me. The more I struggled to free myself the tighter it became wrapped around my legs. Suddenly, my already bound legs were being pulled forward causing my upper body to lunge backwards beneath the water. The fishing wire hindered me from treading water. Now, at that moment, I realized I was fighting for my life.

I slapped violently against the water which this action only allowed me to surface just long enough to gasp deeply taking in air and water. This happened several times until I became so exhausted that giving up became an option.

I remember being so afraid the entire while I was fighting. But the very moment I came to the reality I wasn't going to win this battle on my own, I let go enough to find peace in not struggling. Fear, which was creating such a horrible experience, became replaced by a calmness I still do not understand to this day. When I ceased fear's operation or dictation of my journey, I then suffocated it.

Obviously, since I'm writing about the experience, I made it. When I gave up, I felt a strong hand snatch me up allowing me to regain my footing and hope of survival.

So what am I saying? To reiterate the point about fear's suffocating quality I would equate it with drowning in water. Once submerged in fear, if you panic, fighting or slapping against it is useless. Your only hope of an escape is to use its opposite calmness. Once you have calmed yourself, fear begins to dissipate to the point where you can see a way out, a way to live and not die.

Against fear, calmness is going to be the best weapon to combat such a destructive force. If properly wielded, all opposition becomes manageable as focus tames the beast. When the thought process is clear the impossible seems possible.

Once I heard my pastor use an acronym for focus—Fixated On Christ's Unusual Strength. No longer basing your outcome on your own limitations but relying on the strength of a different source takes a degree of clarity, surrendering, and peace that is detrimental for success. The recognition of not being able to conquer this giant alone and the willingness to act accordingly activates a successful process. Never assume this is going to be pretty. It's not, but it will finish well.

Another reason for the lack of beauty in the process is that the force of fear can be so powerful it causes someone to struggle to be themselves. It produces chaotic moments sent to force you into inappropriately redefining yourself. Instead of walking in power, we'll walk in a suffocating weakness; instead of victory, we're the victim. This is what happens when fear has worn us out by making us work harder than we should. Had calmness been the dominant factor, it would have snatched the power from fear.

Entry Points

Where does this fear come from? It definitely wasn't given to us. Yet we have adopted and welcomed it although we were initially given three other more powerful attributes which will be discussed later in this chapter.

Before we can fully regain power back from fear, we must know a few things about it. First off, the knowledge of how fear entered needs to be obtained.

When correlating fear with drowning, it is established that fear came in through the panic of facing death. This too is the same when it is geared towards your efforts of going after the dream which allows the use of the gift placed within. Your dream can go through the same suffocation which will cause you to panic that you will never be able to do it. This causes you to hasten your efforts. Fast is not always the correct speed to travel.

However, we're going to become more specific with the entry points starting with fear of failure. This one causes those it latches onto to panic when they see failure or even think that it is nearby. No one wants to be seen as the one that stepped out to try something others warned against and flopped at it. Private failure can be handled better than failing in the eyesight of others. After all, you were the only one who knew you did not acquire achievement. However, remember the grip of fear. If you failed privately, it may grip you in a way you never try again much less go public.

With public failure, fear will cause someone to go into seclusion. They hide the dream under the radar hoping the memory of their efforts and failure soon be forgotten. Fear, then, is gaining the power to dictate the dream. With its control, potential will never manifest fully.

On the opposite side, there is the fear of success. This type has someone afraid they will not be able to handle the place of greatness they will land into. They know if they try, success is unavoidable. Not knowing what to expect when they arrive, they allow fear to whisper to them they will not be successful for long or they will be hated as well as lonely once they have arrived at their new destination. It also points to the mishaps and failures of others. This comparative thought process is yet another grip of fear to demobilize you from progress. It is a known fact that there are more average Joes than there are successful, mediocrity crashers. Therefore, fear has coaxed you into believing the tragic lie that you having the potential to do great things is enough.

Another way fear seeps into our chasing efforts is through competition. Panic sets in when the already rushed deadline of a date that was too stringently set is nearing. Remember, fast is not always the speed needed to travel. However, the rush is all about winning against someone who may be unaware they are included in this competition. This action causes a rush of the process, which will never allow the revealing of all the hidden diamonds involved in your project. Thereby the results are exponentially lesser than what could've, should've or would've been obtained had the dream had the time to simmer. In this instance, fear's operation has choked the fullness out of the assignment because of a competition. Run in your own lane by developing the dream that is inside you.

What happens when this competition is on an indirect level? This is when you see people use their children to compete against someone else. They place their children in multiple activities forcing them to achieve and acquire trophies that will give the parent bragging rights to use as a banner of victory against a neighbor, a co-worker, or whomever. The tragedy is that the child is the one suffering by being in activities they may not even like all while thinking the parent is guiding them to do things that would be in their best interest. This type of competiveness not only pushes the child away but also teaches them to stay in places or activities they do not desire to be in just for the sake of doing.

The development and control of fear is a harsh thing to live with once its operation has been realized. The beauty of it is you do not have to live being powerless to fear. It no longer has to control you. Recall the mentioning of the characteristics that you were endowed with before fear took over. These three will be the key to you regaining what was pushed to the back. I urge you to reclaim your power.

Reclaim Your Power

For God hath not given us the spirit of fear, but of power…
2Timothy1:7

Normally when we see fire we launch an attempt to extinguish it some kind of way; fearing its rage if it were to run wild. Fire has the power to ruin everything it touches. Then there are controlled fires set purposefully so it will be helpful not destructive. Controlled or wild, fire has a quality that on sight can evoke one to nervously take notice. Yet Paul encouraged and reminded Timothy *to fan into flames the spiritual gift God transferred to* him. He told him to remember what God had placed in him, which was not the emotion of fear but power.

We have had a way of handing over our power since the beginning of time. God gave it to us at creation but somehow we saw a way to transfer it only to accept something lesser than we were ever called to be; powerful to fearful. Accepting the weaker of the two, we beg for more power, more strength, and more of an ability we have already been equipped with. You have to remember.

Power has a source, which is something far greater than the outcome. What is your source? What fuels your determination? Whatever this source is releases at intervals that are not destructive to the receiver. Too much of anything before certain strengths are obtained can cause a damaging surge with the potential to burn out the destination. If God is the source, He is strategic in the release. You can handle anything that He gives you. You have already been equipped while you are being guided into a designated purpose.

Children, until they are taught, are not dominated by fear. They trust when the circumstances say not too. If their parent tells them to jump off something high and they are going to catch them, they jump in spite of height, gravity and the parent's ability or unknown inability to catch them.

When we exhibit this childlike trust towards God not people, we will begin to reclaim the power he had intended for us to have. His design for us was to walk in victory in every area of our lives. It has already been given to us therefore, we need to remind ourselves of the fact by beginning to practice using it. Go after the things He has placed into you. Reclaim your power. Fan the flames.

AND OF LOVE

For God hath not given us the spirit of fear, but...of love...

Love is such a powerful action that the word says it covers a multitude of sins. The Amplified version adds, *forgives and disregards the offenses of others.* If you have been offended, do not tuck it into your heart; get it away from you as quickly as possible. If you are going to make it on this journey you have to contain love so strong it forgets swiftly and disregards regularly.

Jesus was on the cross with soldiers casting lots for his garment and the ones who put Him there stood by mocking while watching to make sure he dies. If Jesus would have been offended, all the power of the cross, the love for many, would have been lost. Instead He prayed, "Father, forgive them, for they know not what they do."

Love is more than an emotion. It can be put into action. It is so strong and powerful that when we love someone we will sacrifice ourselves for him or her. Do you love God more than the gift or the dream? If your thoughts stuttered or the answer may be "No" then you need to pray for the power to properly prioritize. God must be first over everything. If seeking Him is at the top of all things surely He will add what we need. Remember He is a jealous God and will have no one or nothing before Him. And because He loves us so much, He wants for us to receive the revelation that if we love Him then we will surrender everything and He will give us so much more.

You were given a spirit of love for a reason as well as for this season of Dream Chasing. If it is not intact as it should be, work on it. This is not the time to allow anything but love to rule. You are going to need love when they come against you ridiculing you for your decision to get up to do something with what God gave you. You are going to need love to admit to yourself your own faults and that it was your own fingerprint on your past failures. You are going to need love in every area of your life. It is going to take love for the gift and first and most importantly the Giver to go through certain things without quitting. He would not have given it, love, if it were not necessary.

GUARD YOUR MIND

For God hath not given us the spirit of fear, but...of a sound mind.

"A mind is a terrible thing to waste," was a slogan that I heard when I was child. It was the famous quote from the United Negro College Fund commercials. As you read, I want to introduce to some and reintroduce to others these words to you today. Why would we waste a beautiful mind, which has the possibility to do endless things of greatness on something as minimal as fear? With a sound mind you can think, reason, and understand for yourself. That is the very reason it is added to certain legal documents stating that you are of sound mind. You are acknowledging that you are operating in your full mental capacity to make good decisions. Since the mind is the centralized area decisions are made, then guarding it must become something you are adamant about to prevent the wasting of it.

If the mind can be guarded against things such as fear and its counterparts, the possibility of making it will not be so hard to perceive. You will begin to accept the fact you were instilled with greatness on purpose. You need to know how things are working against you in order to defeat it. The discoveries I have made of how things work is just a starting point for you to mentally dig deeper into the inner workings of how these things operate within your own personal life. So let us call some middle names.

What middle names of fear have we become so accustomed to that they hang around innocently? We allow it to remain and never truly label it for what it really is. There are many middle names it may go by which are just as deadly although we tend not to think so. Moreover, if we do not perceive something as detrimental to us, then we will not treat it as such. The five middle names that I wish to point out, we are so accustomed to them that we accept them just as we do breathing; not taking a second thought until there is a problem. The fatal five as I will nickname them are Worry, Agitation, Apprehension, Anxiety, and my all-time favorite, Shyness. I will move through these rather quickly since once you see the operation of it you will become completely enlightened.

Different stresses have the capability to keep us awake at night preventing the proper rest needed for mental clarity. The tendency comes for us to assume it normal to toss and turn thinking about different concerns which have entered our minds. First name Fear, middle name Worry.

It is never alright to worry. When we are worried about something then we do not trust the potential of our True Source because we have taken over the control ourselves. To guard your mind is to be in complete submission to the point worry does not stand a chance.

Do you ever pace the floor or wring your hands nervously in anticipation of something? It is called Agitation. The reason it is likened to fear is for the simple fact that you are fearful that something will or will not happen. You have to calm yourself to take back the control.

"Be anxious for nothing," is a very popular verse. Becoming involved in Anxiety does the complete opposite of what Paul had instructed. Anxiety tosses a person into a state of unease when they are uncertain about an outcome.

The subtlety of this next one is amazing. We even have other little cute nicknames for it. Jitters, the creeps, the heebie-jeebies, and even the butterflies. It is that feeling we get when we feel as if something unpleasant is about to happen. Despite the nicknames, its name is Apprehension, a form of fear just as the rest.

Finally, as I mentioned earlier, my personal favorite is Shyness. This is the one that I was swarmed with and parts of its residue still pop up from time to time. People are often called shy as if it is a part of their characteristic. Others will call someone timid thinking it to be ok but it is not. Shyness is a form of fear that has a death grip on you so tight that you are too afraid to show up, speak up, or stand up on behalf of what is placed inside of you. This is the ultimate reason you deliberately miss the opportunity to launch the dream. Just as the definition of fear states, there is nothing present to justify you physically being harmed.

When highlighted, these problems have the same consistent underlying factor; a lack of control on our part. Even though how to delete things from your thought pattern is discussed in a later chapter, I would be remised if I do not address it here as well. In order to get rid of things that attempt to come to dominate, you have to constantly focus on getting rid of it. Keep asking yourself what is there to fear. Practice life without these attributes which is poisoning your success. More importantly, recognize the truth of what is in operation. One hundred percent fear and you are better than that.

A Gift?

In order to understand the purpose of a sound mind being a gift given to us by the Creator, you have to understand Paul's reasons for writing it. Timothy was in a crisis; Christians were being murdered and being a leader, Timothy was on the hit list.

Knowing that death is impending, it required something greater than his own mindset. He had to be firm to face the storm without wincing.

Having a sound mind means having discipline. If there is a lack of discipline, self-control, or whatever you want to classify it as, you will not stay the course when the fire gets hot. Neither will you continue to conquer when the seas appear to be smooth sailing. Having your mind made up to go the distance to produce in and out of season will provide what is necessary to have staying power. Discipline feeds you mentally during the famine. You will already know not every day is victorious but it is near as long as you do not prematurely quit. Do not be afraid of when things look horrible and growth eludes you. Forests do not appear overnight. They take seasons to grow.

With a sound mind, you have peace when you should have none due to your mind being made up to stay the course. You are determined to make it; standing firm, solid against the attacks. When you are attacked by thoughts speaking volumes to you that "You can't do this," "Nobody in your family has done anything like this before," and "You're not smart enough," you are going to need the inner part of you to be unmovable. Your heart has to be steady. Your consciousness has to be unshakeable. You cannot do this alone; you have to team up with God who is cheering for you anyway.

Arm yourself with things that are going to surround your mind with a positive line of defense so whenever something does come against you, there is something to take it down before it can take root. Your mind must be guarded by the word of God. Find out what He says about you and your ability and you will have something to stand on. Gather scriptures, songs, quotes etc., to be as mental cues to speedily trigger you back to the right frame of mind. This is what you need to feed your mind whether you are under attack or in a season of peace. Soldiers do not begin training when they get into battle.

When God is on your side, there is no need to fear. He has equipped you with the items necessary to win. Just dig down deep pulling them back to remembrance and go for it as if you know that God is cheering for you.

When I had safely returned to the beach, wounded by the experience of almost drowning, as I shed the fishing wire from my legs, an angry elderly man approached me. I laugh about it today when I realize the source of his anger was that I was not the big catch he thought he was going to be able to brag about. However, then, I gave him a peace of my mind. My anger was far more fierce than his simply due to one element; fear almost won.

Dream Motivator

When you make the decision to live fearlessly, it changes your entire attitude. Begin to look at life from the perspective of what do you have to lose.

What is your biggest fear that leaves you standing still even when you are pumped to trek towards your goal?

_____

Hint: Whatever the answer, delete it after chapter 5.

II. Daily Bread

When I was in the 2nd grade, I would be so excited about what I was learning that as soon as my daddy got home I had to show him everything that we went over in school. At the age of seven with energy in surplus, I did not realize that he was exhausted from working all day long. After a couple of weeks of this, without breaking my spirit, he gave me a new assignment that would make my teaching sessions shorter. He said to me, "Learn enough for the both of us."

Enough to a child means *everything*. This one phrase set me in motion to have a continual desire for learning. At that age, I did what I thought would be enough and that meant reading dictionaries, encyclopedias, and whatever I could get my hands on even if it was beyond my level of comprehension. Meditate on those last five words until I come back to it. However, my daddy did not realize that he created a hunger for learning inside of me simply by issuing a new focus to me. Instead of trying to teach him, learn enough to represent the both of us. That is really the epitome of a great parent; the child is to be better or achieve more than the parent. They give or direct you to what you need to sustain until you can get it on your own.

Are you hungry? If so, to what degree? When your stomach growls at certain octaves, it has a way of getting your attention until you can focus on nothing other than food. In the natural, your hunger is controlling your mind. With your dream, your hunger is controlling your decisions. What are you eating to bring satiety to your efforts?

Therefore, I ask you again. Are you hungry? If so, in this chapter as well as the entire book lie the answers to being fed. There are times in which being hungry is a prerequisite to chasing after your dream. Your appetite is whet for the achievement you so desire almost forcing you to gravitate to stalk mode.

However, the type of hunger being referenced here is on the negative side. When we are hungry it means that we are lacking something that is a necessity, a nutrient that is vital to our existence. For some reason we have not consumed the proper amount at the proper timing sending our stomachs to suffer at the hands of hunger pangs. Yet somehow we are able to continue on until our next meal is obtained if that is at all possible.

In some regions of the world, the next meal may not be as immediate as opening the refrigerator or walking into a restaurant. These are the areas in which the possibility of starvation is sometimes around the corner. Not being able to eat for lengthy periods of time will cause the symptoms of starvation and malnutrition to be seen outwardly.

What does this have to do with Dream Chasing? Everything. There are times in which we are in starvation mode in the things we desire to achieve without recognizing neither the fact we are hungry nor the symptoms. The signs were there but they were missed or attributed to something else. For example, one of the first signs of starvation is fatigue since the body is not being fueled properly. The sign that is easy to miss is the feeling that working on your dream later is better. Whenever putting something off that you enjoy seems to be a means of survival, that is a clear sign of Dream Fatigue.

Other symptoms of natural starvation include the breaking down of muscles, vitamin and mineral deficiency, depression, anxiety, nervousness and impatience. These symptoms can all be correlated with the starvation of your dream. First your energy gets sapped only to lead to the breaking down of your muscles which is your desire to dream. Being vitamin and mineral deficient to your dream is not feeding it the time that you once did which causes you to become depressed. Then anxiety comes in the form of an overwhelming sense of nervousness that if you do not achieve it immediately then it will never happen. Decisions made hastily are not equivalent to the fast track to success. Actually, this swift attempt to make up for lost time can be the seed to a massive setback. The level of impatience grows contributing to more fatigue.

The most interesting symptom of starvation is the one of food obsession. Obsession is when someone can't seem to get enough of something although with food obsession they are not consuming the food yet they are thinking about it, talking about it, and searching for it—constantly. With people that desire to do something in life, when they hit the point of frustration or level of starvation, then they obsess about their dreams although they are not successfully doing anything to make it happen. They may talk about it but not work on it, think about it with no progress, and even search for it to never find it.

When this level of starvation is reached, it is time to eat properly to regain what is needed, what has been lost. Although time cannot be regained does not mean a new arrival time cannot be established. Learn to eat what is nutritionally sound for your desire. In order to keep your strength up, it necessitates eating every day.

A dream chaser and any believer's form of eating what is right is developing a strong prayer life. The one who hungers and thirsts after righteousness shall be filled. My husband taught me a valuable lesson on being consistent with a daily prayer as he is diligent with getting his time in. Prayer is the essential component to eating well. This is the most important meal of the day as well as for any journey that you choose to embark upon. Prayer connects you to a source that is higher than you. Think on how a GPS works. The system in your car connects with an orbiting satellite to download information based on what it sees. Therefore, allow God to download the appropriate instructions into you that will erase the signs of malnutrition getting not only what you dream about to its proper destination but your entire life.

ASK GOD FIRST

A great lesson to learn whenever we are seeking after things in life that our mind has been set apart to desire would be one of humility. Humility says to the inner self, "I do not always have to be the best," or "I do not know everything; there are others that have achieved a greater level of success in the area that I desire to conquer." Humility begins a search for direction from an external source yielding to the truth that if greatness is to be achieved then it, humility must be acquired.

Humility reminds us that we are not better than other people. Being humble enough to ask directions from others was what I learned from my father. He told me that when he was a young adult, before he set out to do something on a large scale, he always asked his dad for advice. After making the statement he then proceeded to detail the characteristics of his advisor listing getting drunk every weekend which led him to sometimes being robbed of his weekly salary in his pocket which in turn forced the family to come together to survive for the following week.

You may ask why he would ask someone like that for advice which was the very question that I had in my mind as well. Before I could ask, my father answered the question. He explained in his own way that when we ask those that are older than or have some kind of rule over us, then we seem to make out better than if we did not. That individual's life may seem to be a wreck however it is about what you do not see or their mental capacity. In this case, being humble would have to take precedence over what you thought about an individual or even over what you think about yourself.

When taking a look at what you want to do, what you desire to chase after and how it seems to be larger than you, how do you figure that you can accomplish something of this magnitude just by relying on internal data. Look around observing closely at nature and how the stars are hung in the sky, why the sun shines like it does, and the order of the seasons. In your observation, question if you could have done this with such perfection.

Now look at your hand or still yourself long enough to feel your own heartbeat, paying close attention to the mechanism of your breathing. Could you have done the same thing with such harmonic accuracy? Even though we could not have done these things, there is One who did and continues to do.

Just as my father asked his father whenever he was about to tackle something big then we too need to ask our Father whenever we are about to chase after the dreams that He has instilled in us. When we ask Him for directions on what to do and how to go about it, we are making the acknowledgement that He is the Creator of everything and the Giver of every good gift. Matthew wrote, "But seek ye first the kingdom of God and His righteousness; and all these things shall be added unto you." God is willing to supply your every need.

Asking God first should be automatic although it is not since for so long we have depended on self to get things done. We worked hard on the job to get the promotion; we forfeited sleep to raise the baby who turned into a high-income generating professional athlete; and the list goes on and on of the things that we have accredited to self. In the midst of humility, we put down what we thought we accomplished to realize that we could not have accomplished any of it had we not had the still small voice speaking to us giving wisdom and directions; our GPS was connected.

It takes time to detox our way of doing things to form new habits but consider this a necessity if you are hungry. Humility is surrendering which takes practice and lots of effort especially when you either do not want to or you do not understand the reason for it. In surrendering, by its definition, you are making an agreement to stop fighting, hiding, or resisting because you know that you will not win or succeed; you are giving control over. Look at it from this perspective. When you give up or surrender to God the things we hold valuable to our hearts, then we will see transference of responsibility from self to Him.

It doesn't take a lot of strength to hang on. It takes a lot of strength to let go—J C Watts

Now from a corrected mindset, you now know to ask God first in all things. If the importance level of what you dream about is high enough then you will recognize the fact you do not want to risk botching it up. Last time you went into starvation mode; this time you must do something different.

When we ask God things concerning our dreams and lives, we are submitting to Him as being sovereign, ruler over everything, and supreme in all wisdom and knowledge. In James 1:5(NLT) it states, "If you need wisdom, ask our generous God, and He will give it to you. He will not rebuke you for asking."

With knowing that He will not rebuke you for asking for directions, then feel comfortable enough to let your request be made known. Your actions are telling the Father that you need Him and His infinite directions; you can't do it without Him. As my own father said, just by him asking his dad, it made him feel needed despite his mishaps. So when the Heavenly Father sees that you need Him, be encouraged to know He is going to overtake you with what you need when you need it.

When you ask God for directions it does not have to be a long, drawn out, complicated request in a form of language you are not comfortable speaking. Don't try to sound like the Bible; sound like yourself. Keep it simplistic, straightforward, and not too vague for your sake. If it is too vague when you ask, chances are you will miss the answer when it comes. Ask based on what you have been given. And remember to never get to the point of only asking for things concerning what you are trying to accomplish for yourself, but always pray for others as well. Also, pray to continue a relationship with the Father and to have a spirit of humility.

My final point for this section is to be like David especially when regardless of your skills, heart, and passion level, the situation seems to be too much for you to handle. That is when your once champion ally due to circumstance is now your equally as deadly opposition. You are caught between a rock and a hard place where you really do not know how you will make it through this. This particular difficult situation is enough to make you quit but something on the inside keeps saying the fight is not over.

"So David inquired of the Lord, saying, "Shall I pursue this troop? Shall I overtake them?" –I Samuel 30:8

There has to be a place in your mind where you quiet the chaos with your most effective weapon—prayer. David asked up since he needed to tap into his GPS. The answer David received has been motivation to me so many times especially when I was in a place where I felt my opportunity had been hijacked and taken captive. When I asked up just as David, I was either released to go recover it all or redirected to elsewhere. Whatever the answer, due to me asking God, I came out victorious and so will you.

DECIPHER THE GIFTING

As you already have what you want to go after before you, think more deeply on what you have been given. Just as the dream has been instilled within you, the gifting to make it happen has been also. When the term gifting is used, it is speaking of the special ability or talent that has freely been given to an individual; it cannot be worked for or earned. If you work to acquire it, then it becomes a skill or trade. However, do not confuse that with thinking you are not to work to increase or improve what you have been given.

Look at the following examples to differentiate between gifting and skill. Emma was 2-years old when she sat at the piano and amazingly began to play without ever having a lesson. Tara always wanted to play the piano, so she paid for lessons until she learned how to play. Emma is the example of gifting as playing the piano was something that was in her already whereas Tara is an example of a skill acquired by learning from an external source.

With those two examples in mind, take a look at your dream. Now look at some of your attributes that would be helpful to you acquiring the dream. Are your findings a gifting or a skill that you've acquired over time? If you find that you have been gifted with something as well as given the passion to accomplish a dream, then you need to take a deeper look at what you have been given and why.

Sometimes we think the desires we own are just something that has always been prevalent when in fact those desires were given to us sometimes as even far back as birth. It becomes your job when you come into the knowledge you have a gifting to interpret why you have been entrusted with this trait along with how and when are you to use it effectively. Finding the answer to those questions would continue the theme of asking God especially since you had no power over what was placed in you. You are going to have to ask up to decode this special ability.

One of my favorite bible characters is David. David was killing bears and lions when he was young and keeping sheep. When he got older, he killed a giant. Then when he got even older, he was killing soldiers by the thousands. But there came a time that something was outside of his wits to know what to do; the city had been burned, the family taken, and he had 600 hundred equally ruthless soldiers ready to kill him. His first thing to do was to enquire of the Lord although he was gifted as a warrior. Had he acted on his own wisdom, he probably would have met his demise. However, when he asked God, he was shown exactly what to do plus the ones that had turned against him were now back on his side as he followed the advice of God to successfully recover all of their substance.

Remember this story when you enquire of the Lord for your own life. The gifting to come against things that were bigger than himself was always inside of David growing as he grew in time, knowledge and skill. Yet David was humble enough to ask God instead of looking at his own gifting to be a warrior. That last statement leads me to my next point on gifting. Earlier I made the statement about gifting being freely given but skills are learned. Do not be confused when you look back over your gifting to see how it grows. You are born with bones inside your body yet as you grow, so do they. The gifting is the same way unless you starve it.

Before you realized your gift, it found a way to feed on its own until you came to the knowledge of how to do so. It found a way to get the daily bread that it needed to survive until its purpose would be served. You probably thought the things you experienced were coincidental until you looked deeper at the root of it all. Your gifting was strengthening and growing based on a destination that you had no knowledge of.

Determine the Destiny

Destiny is all a part of what is going to happen or what will be experienced some time in the future. It is not always possible to pinpoint with accuracy the exact time an event will happen such as the birth of a child. However, based on the knowledge that something is happening, you can structure the experience to where it benefits you better in the end. Some people haphazardly stumble upon success while others strive for it. Success was their destiny although they did not know exactly when but they planned for it to happen.

Planning for future events can sometimes be frustrating but when you have determined that it will be something great it can be transformed into quite a rewarding experience. Knowing an estimated destination helps astronomically when you have to push past what you see as being not so great or so rewarding. Most often the middle part of your journey is not always known with the beginning and the ending showing a bit more clearly. Going after something requires you to start from scratch or from where you are currently to achieve something so compounded that you cannot even fathom how to get there on your own.

So often people fool themselves by thinking that this journey is going to be a piece of cake. After getting along into it, they begin to realize their fallacy. This recognition causes too many to give up when they look certain oppositions in the face. Sometimes a hurt overcomes them because what they dreamed the ending would be looked far worse than what they were experiencing. However, when you determine the destiny, you will begin to seek out certain types of things to happen and you will not be robbed of your motivation that you began with.

A means of encouragement is to find out that where you are going is closely connected to where you are now and where you have been. So if you take a look back over your life, happiness and frustrations alike, you can see some of the places where you will end up. There are times in which things happen in life that forgetting them would be what we see as the best thing for us. However, forgetting sometimes leaves out pieces of the puzzle. Pick up the pieces, place them together, to help you see clearer.

The farther backward you can look, the farther forward you can see—Winston Churchill

Genesis 37 starts the story of Joseph, the beloved son of Jacob. In his story, there are a number of events in his life that he would have happily pushed to the outsides of his mind but they were all powerfully apart of his journey. The destiny connected to the dream, that once told, catapulted him into a chain of events that he would have never foreseen. The only thing he saw was the amazing ending of the dream, not the ugly middle. The only way he made it was by holding onto who he was, his God, and the dream.

One of the keys to your success is going to be just like Joseph. Never forget who God made you to be. This is the only way to get what He has for you. When determining what you have and what it will become, you will be devising a road map to get you from point A to point B. Regardless of whether you are using a paper map or a high-tech GPS, you will not see the potholes or the bumpiness of the surface that you have to travel. You just know that you have to get there at all cost. Finishing is necessary. Failure is not an option. This time…this time you are determined to make it to the point of your destiny. You have eaten well and are all fueled up for where you have to go.

Dream Motivator

Every day make a decision that regardless of how remarkable and self-sufficient you are that you will seek God first in everything. When you first open your eyes upon a new day, surrender and watch how wonderful life turns out.

III. Declare It

"You will also declare a thing, and it will be established for you..."
—Job 22:28

Declaration is a special act. Not everyone has the guts to accomplish this. It takes heart and courage to declare something with expectancy without knowing how it is going to happen. Even further, when faith connects to the heart, what has been declared has a way of driving an individual. The person who speaks something knowing it shall be established is an uncommonly extraordinary individual. That is why you are reading this book—you know the greatness inside of you is different in a special way.

Although it takes an extra push to get to this level, you need to applaud yourself for just being brave enough to have the desire to enter into this club. This is the same club that self-made millionaires belong to. The same club that highly accomplished athletes pays their membership dues to belong. The same club the debt free, the successfully married, the mentor, and countless others who dared to dream happily belong. This is the same area anyone that has a success story has and must visit if they wish to be more than common.

One day, I was listening to the story of a successful playwright that seemed to have obtained success overnight. The more he spoke the more I realized that overnight success is a fairytale. The process that gets you to achieve the uncommonly extraordinary story can be slowly excruciating. Yet in the end, it is worth every moment of discomfort. How bad do you want it?

CALL THE SHOT

David, before he was a mighty warrior, kept his father's livestock. This was a job he took on due to his position as the youngest of the family. Keeping the animals was not a job that gained a lot of glory; it was common and did not take a lot of effort so it would seem. David had a fighter inside of him who had to be humbled down to keep the sheep until the battle designed for him was ready to be fought.

Sometimes, we take on jobs that do not challenge us bringing about the feelings of a misplaced destiny. Those jobs are looked upon as only a means of supplying an income until our big day of doing what we know we were designed for arrives. However, those are the jobs we gain the training of how to excel with grace and gain promotions without pride. Never look at the temporary assignment as a waste of time but as growth and learning. While you are in training know that there are appointed times in which who you are right now will collide with who you will become. This is the time to call the shot.

David visited the camp where the Army of Israel was being taunted by a giant. Seeing the fearful morale of the soldiers, he became stirred up enough to begin asking questions. There were those that knew him, his brothers, who thought he could do nothing here since he was a sheep keeper. Perhaps there was a time when they themselves kept the sheep so they discredited his ability in war not realizing that he was accustomed to defeating things larger than himself.

After getting the information he needed, David took the challenge to be the one to face this giant. There was a lot more at stake than just being defeated; if they lost, they would become the slaves to the opposing nation. Future freedom was on the shoulders of a shepherd boy who had more heart than stature.

Are you seeing yourself in this? Have you recalled times in which the things that you declared have led you to be discredited by those who think that you are incapable of doing what you have said? Keep this next statement close to mind at all times. Declaration is not only about what you speak can happen; your speech must desperately, fervently connect with your heart. For when the battle gets tough, it takes heart to press through the storm that your mouth got you into. This is your dream, so call the shot.

David went out against a giant that was yelling unpleasantries toward him. What did David speak in return? He called the shot; he made the decision of the course of action. David spoke exactly what he was going to do to this giant that dare defy the God of Israel and his words manifested giving him the victory. You too must call the shot when you make a declaration.

DEFINE THE DREAM

Let there be light…and there was. The Creator gave His words a particular assignment. Not only did He declare, but also He directed His words to accomplish what He knew they could be. They became epic. An entire universe, all of creation was resting on the breath of God Almighty. That same breath, He exhaled it into the dust of the ground creating a living being to witness the power of His words. What does the breath He breathes into you give life to? What is the definition of your inner desire?

What you dream is up to you. Just as differently as people are created so too are the things we desire. You should not base your dreams on what other people expect from you or on what others are doing. What is good for one is not necessarily good for everyone. If we are to be contributors to the whole plan then there has to be some difference. What is God speaking voluminously to you to accomplish?

Just as you have called the shot you must also define your dream. It is up to you to determine the meaning of what you are chasing after. The more that you dig into its meaning the more you will be shaping and outlining specific aspects of it causing clarity to come more to you. Sitting down to do this now will sustain you when things get tough.

Questions you should ask yourself and God start with what is the purpose of your particular assignment? Is it for you; who will it benefit? Everything that has been downloaded into you is not for your individual purpose. There are things that you desire that ultimately benefit others. Even if it is not about you, you have to be okay with that and have the same passion to press through when the battle gets hot.

Often stories of people's lives are told where they had a vision for their life that did not altogether line up with what they thought it would be. Their primary goal was for the benefitting of self yet after it was completed the more rewarding part was that they made the sacrifice having others benefit from their push. Think about motivational speakers. They go through things they really would not wish to in order to get a word to give to uplift others. In the end, not only did others develop something greater from their hardship, but they themselves transformed into a greater person.

Continuing with your questioning will help you to learn the boundaries and limits of your dream. How far will it go? What areas will it reach? What kind of impact will it have? Not all questions will be answered at the beginning. They will be supplied as you go along and when it is most needed.

Soon you will begin to see the character of your dream distinguish itself from other people's dreams as well as other things you desire. Your choices will be determined by its character as you discover more of your dream's qualities. Details will begin to clearly outline a plan for you to follow. As you go along, there will be other questions that come to you that will be helpful. The questions are specific to the dream and the destiny. Ask wisely.

GIVE YOUR DREAMS A DESTINATION

Where are you going? My husband likes to go to the track to run. I, on the other hand, cannot stand it. It is something about running in circles that I just cannot get with. Now if you give me a scenic route, I can take that better. However, when he is running, he wants me to time him. Although he is going in a circle his destination is a time; he is trying to beat his former record. If there was not a place that he was trying to get to then he would be aimlessly running which could be tiring. There is a clear-cut goal set for his running; beat the previous time.

When a destination is set, you can cater your mind to go towards it. Just as his destination was not a geographical location neither will yours be all the time. It is the personal goal you have set forth for yourself. It is the place inside your mind, your details which will signify you have arrived. It is the place to reach where you feel the tape at the finish line snap across your chest.

With your goal being different from the next person's, so will your destination. I cannot stress this enough. It will be a tragic thing to think you have reached your finish line to only figure out you have become a carbon copy of someone else. A shudder should come over you to remember all the hard work, sacrifice, and lost time spent to arrive at a place that will yield neither gratification nor completion. The dream will still hauntingly beckon you to chase after it.

I will ask again. Where are you going? If you have no idea, then revisit what you have declared, what you have spoken to come into existence. The destination must be held before you at all times so that you will know when you get off course. Joseph's place of destiny was to be in charge with his family bowing to him. That much he knew. So when he is in charge at Potiphar's house, he knew he hadn't arrived because his family was not there to confirm it. So he had to keep moving or rather the goal kept moving him. Even though he wound up being important wherever he went, including the palace, the tape did not snap across his chest until his brothers came to him in need. Dream manifested.

I WAS VS I AM

> *"...calls those things which do not exist as though they did..."*
> —Romans 4:17

This particular scripture describes Abraham's faith before he received the promise. He had hope even though what he was seeing did not constitute him to. He trusted God solely based on what God had spoken; what God had breathed into him; multitude of lives coming from the barren and elderly. Faith so strong he defied what he was currently to believe what the Great I Am said he was to become.

There are times in which we hold onto the past tense version of ourselves bringing it into our present time robbing us of the chance to become greater. We hold "I was" up to be more credible than "I am." It is though there is an automatic migration towards the negative part, which had not experienced growth yet. Almost as if a refusal to see the greatness that has been placed on the inside. When you change what ministers to you, then you will be able to go forth in a mighty way. It is time to change.

I was is a past tense phrase placed in front of some characteristic or state of being to fingerprint our part that was played in a particular event in life. This stamp continues on until it is replaced with something else, a better hallmark that is noted to cancel out the previous statement. This is where the phrase I am takes over.

I am is current with whatever following it having a certain degree of power to change the outcome. Whatever is put behind those two simple words need to be done so with expectation; calling it to be. When we have enough faith, like Abraham, to believe even though we do not see, then we will begin to see some mighty things happen in our lives.

Have you ever heard people speak who suffered but survived a terrifying illness? Pay close attention to the word usage of their testimony? They would say, "I was so sick but I believed God for my healing." Although their current state, the pain racking through their body and all the symptoms of an illness, clearly stated they were not healed yet there had to be a moment an inner change occurred giving them something hopeful to hold onto. In the middle of sickness, they begin to declare, "I am healed."

History yields many great examples of people who went against the grains life was throwing them to wind up doing some remarkable things. There comes a time in which you have to use someone else's testimony to find strength until you can make the affirmation for yourself. Joseph could have said, "I was in the pit," even while he was making progress. If he would have kept holding onto the pity of the pit experience, how could he have enjoyed his "but I am in the palace," victory?

There was even a time in which you tried after the very thing you are holding dear to your heart now. In the back of your mind,

"I was a failure", "I was unsuccessful" continuously repeats hammering down the will to state what you will become—successful. There may be people, dream killers, who constantly bring the past to your remembrance. Those negative words can ring louder than the positive but I dare you to declare your victory right now. Make your "I am" statement. Let that be what is repetitious to the point you begin to migrate towards it. It is inevitable that you release one to receive the other.

This is the time to shake off yesterday to run with today. Do not remind yourself of your past failures but remind yourself of your positive future. Grab hold to the power of I am. If no one else believes in you, I do and more importantly, God does.

Dream Motivator

Declaration is not only about what you speak can happen; your speech must desperately, fervently connect with your heart. For when the battle gets tough, it takes heart to press through the storm that your mouth got you into. This is your dream. So call the shot.

My Declaration:
_____
_____

My "I Am" Statement:
_____
_____

IV. Dangle the Dream Before You

What do you envision your dream will become? How do you plan to get there? These are just samples of questions you will find necessary to keep before you constantly. It is not enough to only make a declaration, but you must keep yourself continuously motivated. Whatever you have before you is what you will become.

Jacob wanted separation from his father-in-law Laban to be able to take care of his own family. He had a proposition for Laban that he would continue to care for his sheep but he would receive the spotted or streaked sheep and goats. Laban agreed, secretly having his sons remove all of the sheep and goats Jacob would have received. However, during mating season, when the strong sheep would come to drink water, Jacob would place a peeled tree bark that was spotted, speckled or streaked before them. And what they saw affected what they conceived. When they gave birth the newborn would be one of the three that was seen by the conceiving mother.

Wherever you are trying to go, or whatever you wish to accomplish, place it before you so that when you conceive it in your mind and your heart, the rest will follow.

MENTAL CUES

Song lyrics, when pondered upon, have a way of swaying the mood of its listener. It audibly inspires someone to either be happy or sad, motivated or depressed. Yielding subconsciously to a melody, fingers begin tapping steering wheels while heads in a carefree manner bounce to the rhythm entering their ears. Every song does not have the same affect upon individuals. What moves one person is just as unique as the goals that are set. The key point is that inspiration to do something came from what you heard. This is an audible mental cue.

There are things that are going to inspire each of you differently. To get up in the morning, you may need an upbeat song to make you jolt out of bed to head toward your dream as if your life depended upon it. Or perhaps it's a slow song that you need to wind down so that you can focus on planning your next step. Whatever inspires you has to be chosen by you.

In the Spring of 2012, I decided to finish writing a novel I had started but lagged around on. I knew I needed a little extra boost. Just listening to the radio one day, I heard the perfect song because it moved me in a way all the other music I had heard did not. Seeking the song out, I came across another by the same artists which had the same affect. After downloading the songs, I began religiously listening to them before I would write. It was not long before I had a full rough draft in my hand all because of what I dangled before me.

Then there are the times in which inspiration comes visually just as it was in the example of the sheep. Perhaps a poster hangs over your desk with a phrase or quote on it when read ushers in the possibility of accomplishment. The feelings of this being the time overcomes you in a way you actually believe it. Great advice would be to say if it moves you, be sure to keep it before you. This does not always have to be a purchased item. Your own personally inspiring quote may be the trigger for you to dig deeper. It only takes minutes to create, print, and hang.

Be inventive when it comes to bringing inspiration before you. When something moves you to go farther, keeping it before you at all times will prove beneficial to your efforts.

DISCOVER THE PASSION

Passion for a goal is what drives people to stay longer, be stronger, and fight harder. Without passion, weariness is around the corner along with the possibility of throwing in the towel after the first wave of opposition.

It is amazing what individuals can do when they are passionate about something. It is seen in their eyes, heard in their speech, and manifests in their actions. When people love what they do, they become a force to be reckoned with. They become unstoppable.

With the correct level of devotion, defending the dream comes just as second nature as protecting a child. This emotion must be the intense ruling force pushing the dream with the capability to negate any potential failure. That is why you must feed passion often.

The more planning placed into your dream chasing, the more excitement you will feel arising within you. Already asking questions, you begin to receive answers that will allow you to progress along. The more advancement being made means completion is nearing. It is my recommendation to compose a Dream Book; something to notate the process of your journey.

Whenever I think about a Dream Book, my attention turns to the scripture that reads, "Write the vision, and make it plain on tablets, that he may run who reads it." Write the vision to see the vision. Make whatever you are going after plain enough that it excites, motivates and inspires.

Compiling a Dream Book is simple as the materials needed are few. Use a ring binder or any notebook where pages can be added or taken away. Fill it with paper and tabs to section off different aspects of your goal. This will be more or less like a very detailed and organized journal with dates and transactions in it. By organizing your Dream Book it will cause a couple of things to happen. One will be that you will notice your love for what you are doing will increase whenever you open it thumbing through the pages looking at your notes. The second is that you will gain knowledge of future steps since you are detailing your plan. You will not know all the steps but sit and think what your next move could possibly be yet keeping an open mind if any changes should need to be made.

Figure out what sections need to be inside your book for the particular goal you have in mind. I will use myself as an example. When I created my Dream Book there were several things I wanted to accomplish. Some of them have been completed; some have not. One of the dreams in the book is being an author. Under that section I have subsections such as book titles, word counts, hours spent writing with the date, and time doing research. This way I can look back to see how many hours I spent writing a particular book. It was something about doing this that encouraged me to plop down in from of the computer to write. I knew I would have to make another entry, which showed progress.

Also, create a Dream Board. This board could be chalk or dry erase in which you jot down quick notes and memos for yourself to see the moment you walk into the area this is set up. This is where your to-do list will go and any notes reminding you of meetings or things you need to do. With it being on a wall and not in a book, these are quick notes that will be changed out often. Place something on the board encouraging pertaining to the goal you have in mind.

All of these things are designed to keep you seeing the vision. When you are constantly reminded of where you are going, then getting there becomes obvious and not so much a task. You are training yourself to become what you already feel you have on the inside; the passion to become successfully you.

Dream Motivator

Whatever it is you are attempting to achieve, keep it before you constantly. You may not have a piece of paper or a Dream Book with you at all times. However, your brain is always there. Think on that.

V. Delete and Defeat Your Demons

Demon? I know your mind may have ventured to the horror movies you have seen about people who are demonically possessed in which their bodies become distorted and they growl in voices that do not belong to them. Your next thought probably was that you don't have anything like that living within you or at least you hope not.

However, the demon I am speaking about is just as terrifying. It torments you, distorting your desire to chase after your dream. Instead of living the life you were destined to, you are living one that belongs to someone else. Your demon has been very effective in distracting you away from your true purpose. Yes! You have a demon.

By definition, something that causes a person to have a lot of trouble or unhappiness is a demon. Surely, you have had some trouble or some times of unhappiness, but what was the source? There are some people who can do the job of causing unhappiness really well but that does not make them a demon although some act as if they are possessed. Here, we want to look at what was the internal cause of the things going wrong with you? What is your personal demon?

REVEALING THE PROBLEM

When it is time to look inside ourselves to consider our ways, it becomes onerous. Clearly, no one wants to be a contributing factor to their own lack of success. It is easier to accept downfalls coming from the external source of someone who does not want to see you succeed. That is the case some of the time. However, all bases need covering to prevent any further delays when it comes to reaching the goal. Being your own hindrance is something most people do not want to admit, but for the sake of advancement, this step cannot be avoided. Let's look in the mirror.

There are times in which you may not be aware of how to recognize where the demons are in your life that fight against your dream. This is where you have to focus and take notes. You need to jot down your actions as if you are outside of your own body doing an observation. Please do not justify your activities; write them all down. It could be one item that is meaningful but done too long or too many times outside of necessity could be what is dragging your success down.

Here is an example of a writer using social media which is imperative for them to reach their audience. Done too often, the time they should have spent writing is sapped up leaving them wondering why they could not finish the very book in which the audience is waiting for. Their inability to productively use social media is their demon; the thing keeping them from fruition.

Now here is a list of things designed to provoke you to think about how and why these items are considered demons. Use this same list to focus on how to find the ones that are specific to you. The underlying traits for most demons are they have the ability to still, kill or destroy your progress. Once you read the word *still* instead of steal a red flag should have went up in your mind. I purposely wrote that word because it is those times in which your demon causes you to halt and you don't even recognize it. In addition, there will be things that are distractions or attempts to redirect your purpose. In that, I mean look for things that try to get you off track or make an effort to persuade you to try something other than what you have in your heart. These can be so subtle they become extremely easy to miss. Be sure to pull out a fine-tooth comb when searching for these. Keep these forewarnings before you as you begin your self-check.

Procrastination and laziness are demons. Whenever things are put off until a later time without a feasible explanation, then you have a problem. Not only does it occur once, but also it is habitual. An excuse always seems to present itself giving a really good reason to putting off working towards the goal.

Fear and doubt are demons. If you find yourself being apprehensive about doing the things that you so love, then you have a problem with fear. Somewhere along the lines anxiety seeped in making you afraid that you are going to either fail or succeed. There is nothing to fear but the mental battle incompletion or quitting will submerge you into. And doubt has a way of siphoning confidence out of your heart making you question who you are and why you thought you could accomplish this goal. Put the two together and they will completely drain you of the strength to even attempt something outside of the ordinary.

Offenses, grudges and the inability to forgive are all demons that holds its victim in a bondage whereas they not only fail at the goals they desire but also find it difficult in what used to be the more simplistic areas of life. You are held captive by what you are holding on the inside towards someone else not realizing it is eating away at your life like Stage 4 Cancer. The longer you hold onto them, the more destructive they are.

Are you always busy with a lot of different tasks with a considerable amount of them being for others? That is busyness camouflaged as helpfulness and charity. Yes. Busyness is a demon.

Why are you so busy? Busyness is one letter away from doing business yet instead you pile task after meaningless task onto a plate ladened with fat and other things lacking any nutritional value keeping you in a bondage that is designed to arrest you from developing into the person you are purposed to be. Your dream is dying in a state of malnutrition simply because you are busy.

Why are you being busy? Is it that you don't want to hurt anyone's feelings or let someone down by not taking on the task? Or is it that you like the attention afforded you by being the one who will accept the job putting much effort into it until completion? You are overwhelming yourself for the attention of someone who just wants the work done caring less who does it. Here is why you are B.U.S.Y. You are senselessly Being Under Someone's Yoke. If this is you, here's a key phrase you need to learn. It is one simple yet very powerful word called NO. Free yourself of that demon and stop being busy enough to transform that energy into effectively doing business.

Self-sabotage is the type of demon that is very sneaky, covertly hiding in a way discoverability is almost impossible. It hides behind your obliviousness to its vices. It may take you years to figure out you were the one who deliberately derailed your own dreams. Subconsciously you destroyed your own vision for whatever reason is unknown. Maybe it coupled with one of the other demons, as they are known to work in groups, and it utterly subverted your plans of success. If you have a fear of speaking in public somehow something haphazardly happens to keep you from showing up to deliver the speech. In the corner of your mind, you willed something to happen and fate followed. Self-sabotage. Look closely. Look deeply.

This list could get longer but it is dependent of your specific demons that you have. Weed them out so you can find out what to delete in order to find the success you so greatly desire.

DELETE AND DEFEAT

Light has been shown upon the things holding back your success. Now it is time to do something about it. Look at your list of undesirable traits plus the list of things gathered from your self-observation and begin to mentally prepare yourself for the removal of them. To cease doing them, putting the action in reversal is the only way to get rid of these negative attributes. And the caveat here is that it is easier said than done.

Some say it takes just 21 days to break a habit. As you look over the things you are trying to transform out of you will notice it has been a part of you a long time. This is a microwave generation and we like everything instantly. I'm not going to present to you a short time frame to make you falsely believe it will be gone that soon. Yet, hold onto the possibility of it since your diligence is going to play a major role in this transformation. How long it takes to get rid of these things is up to you.

First off, do not try to get rid of everything at the same time. Put it into manageable chunks so you do not overwhelm yourself causing you to give up on all of it. You have already made the important step of recognizing and admitting that you were bothered by these traits.

Next you want to constantly remind yourself of the repercussions of allowing that habit to stay in existence; it's the main cause of you not completing your goals. Ask yourself how did it benefit you in the past and what will be the benefits once it is gone. Do not become flabbergasted to realize some of these demons were actually providing what you thought to be a good benefit. Look at it from this angle; if it was not profiting you anything you would not have held onto it. Therefore, expect some setbacks. Do not beat yourself up for them but just arm yourself with awareness of what to avoid the next time around. Keep going.

At some point in time, it will become easier to live without the negative traits, which will be the perfect time to defeat them, overcome them, and win the victory. If this is going to be done, you will still have to continue periodic self-observations keeping up with advances and/or setbacks noting the situations that tripped you up.

Be sure that when you have removed something that it is replaced with something positive; form good habits. If procrastination was the demon that lived in your house, now that it is clean, move in promptness. As humans, we have a tendency to do better if we are held accountable. Therefore, find someone who will do this task well.

Once you were bothered by these demons but now you are well on your way to being a successful dream chaser who has overcome those inner hindrances making the external ones easier to deal with. It is always harder to change self but now you have been equipped with what to recognize, what to do, and how to delete and defeat it to become the best you possible.

Dream Motivator

Now that you are free of the things holding you back, stay free so you may soar. You have the victory!

My Demon(s):
_____
_____

My Release Date(s):
_____
_____

VI. Don't Tell It; Live It

He who guards his mouth and his tongue keeps himself from troubles—Proverbs 21:23AMP

You have been inspired with a great goal you feel as if you are going to accomplish. It is so exciting just to have the idea downloaded into you through no efforts of your own; you were just sitting there and boom. The idea unfolded exponentially. With your heart racing, you reach for the phone to tell someone. After all, you just want to bounce this great idea you got from God off on someone to see what it sounds like to another person.

As soon as Joseph mentioned his dream it brought more discord from the very individuals who already had something against him. It heightened to the point where thoughts of killing him looked for opportunities until one was found. His brothers did not kill him but their actions had the potential to kill any dream that he had. *"Let's see what becomes of those dreams now,"* were their haughty words as they thought they had the power to defeat what God had given to Joseph.

His story is an example of the trouble one can get into when spilling the beans so to speak, displaying what has been given inwardly. Be prudent with what comes out of your mouth. If you are going to be effective in being a go getter then it is imperative that you learn the who, what, when, where and why of telling the dream.

Who?

Who you tell your dream to should be just as picky of a decision as who you would entrust with your newborn baby. Is this person going to handle it properly; are they going to add nutritional value to you or your dream? Who you tell could mean life or death to your newborn concept. In a perfect world, the ones who are supporters would outweigh those who are adversaries. Since the operations of this world is far from being perfect, just understand there will be some to support, some who come against, and some who are just null and void not caring one way or the other. Be careful.

The chapter on Dream Protection will clearly detail people who you should not tell; those who want to murder your ability to dream. However, there are more people you should not tell and it is not to say they are bad people but it is just that there needs to be a certain level of growth before you begin revealing what you have. Your very own exposure of what you have could be developing people to come against you.

There is a phrase I have heard come out of many peoples' mouths; read it in a plethora of posts on social media platforms as if it were the new thing to do. *My Haters*. I now laugh at the fact of how I have allowed those two words to bother me so much but I think on things from a different perspective now. My platform was that haters do not exist until we create them or empower them to come against us. After gaining new knowledge, I have become aware that there are haters predestined to come against, dislike, and attempt to thwart your efforts the very moment you do something out of the box. My question is since they are already coming, why do some individuals have the strong desire to have a hater? Does that mean they have not accomplished anything to put them on the radar of a hater? Just a question to ponder on.

Some of the things that are done in our lives are going to happen whether we have an audience or not. God has already predestined certain events to take place. With that mindset, I think of how to get there with the least amount of trouble possible. *Developing or inviting* haters is not the type of drama that is necessary. Should they develop without any help from you then consider that something God is allowing to get you to the right place and to bring this negative audience so they can witness His glory.

How are haters developed? It is when boasting of what great idea God has given you keeps being repeated. You may call it bouncing an idea but the more it happens the more it is labeled as boasting in the ears of the one hearing it. Allow me to give you another angle to see this from. If you are telling what God has given you, consider that maybe He has not whispered anything to the one you are conversing with for whatever reason and you with your multiple grand ideas being fired off like a machine gun brings them into the awareness that He has not said one single word to them.

If God did not tell you to release what He has given, then you are creating opposition who could very well rise up against you one day. Even if they do not rise up against you, the possibility of them being offended enough to not support you is definitely sitting front and center.

With all the people in the world quite surely there should be someone who can be trusted. Sure there is. Be spirit led at all stages. Search your heart for reasons for the need to tell. And if you reveal it before the appropriate season, be ready for some trouble. The power of life or death is in that very small member of the body called your tongue.

What and Why?

Information is a very powerful weapon. It can either be used as a tool to help build or it can be used as a weapon to tear down. Kingdoms have been destroyed merely by the information obtained about it from an outside opposing force. Dreams have been crushed by what has been given about its innermost workings.

What you are saying about your goals to others could be the very thing that is hindering it. Although certain things should have already come to pass, it is on delay causing you to pace the floor waiting its arrival. This delay could be the result of some information you have shared about what you were doing. Why did the need to share even arise?

There are questions that will pop into your head with an answer soon to follow. If choosing to smother these valuable pieces of information out of fear of what will be discovered about self, then the result will be what it always has been; no accomplishment. Embrace the truth so moving on and forward will become a bright part of the growth process.

Revisit a time in the past when you shared something about what you were working on. Did feelings of great joy overcome you almost to the point in which you felt you had already arrived? Then perhaps what you are dealing with is a need to feel appreciated or accomplished thereby telling what you are striving for is a way to achieve the desired gratification before putting in the work. The only problem with that is the dream has been revealed in its infancy with no ways of protecting itself from the impending attack.

Or have you shared details about what you were working on so that others will think you are farther along than you are? *If they think that I'm working even though I'm stuck, they will think I'm successful.* Sorry to be the bearer of bad news but every tree is known by the fruit it bears. If there is no fruit then the tree is either not at the stature to start bearing or there is no tree.

Or, finally, were you talking about your latest project to get the confirmation of someone else. This person has been given the power to receive or veto something that God told you to do. What if you were really sent to confirm some things in their life to get them jump-started?

This information you are sharing to receive some internal satisfaction is the very thing being used to keep you out the winner's circle. It can be a hard pill to swallow after finding out that the lack of progress you are experiencing was initiated by your own tongue.

Remember, if God is cheering for you, then you do not need to feel the praise or confirmation of others. Your gift is going to bring Him glory and you will receive your reward for your part in it. He is confirmation enough.

WHEN AND WHERE?

Now when the dream which has been exposed out of season comes under attack, it dries up causing a dread to replace desire. Noticeably, the following phrases become prevalent; "The devil is fighting against me" or "I must be on to something because of the attack" or "This can't be God ordained because it wouldn't be so hard if it was." No. The attack is all because God is possibly attempting to get you to receive the revelation of that a season of silence can work in your favor. He will give you practice with minor things before He trusts you with something major. Learn to zip it. Silence ushers in the big things.

Reconstruct your thinking to search out the appropriate time and place to reveal all things. Have you ever taken notice of people who obtain something great but you never heard a word about it until they had it. Keeping the process quiet is not equivalent to you being afraid of the enemy. Quietness is the equal to maturity. Maturity knows how to accomplish things under the radar until the time and place are appropriate. There is no better platform than the one set by the Almighty

Remember when Joseph first talked about his dream with joy and excitement in his heart, he was young. By the time he had evolved into being second in command of an entire nation, when he recognized his brothers, he kept quiet until certain conditions had been met. This was an older, wiser version of Joseph who had been taught by the best teachers called adversity and experience. Learn from his story so that you will not have to take the hardest course towards living your dream.

Dream Motivator

Regardless of what happens or how bad they hurt you, never carry a spirit of bitterness. Bitterness brings you down to their level. If you do find yourself bitter change the letter and become better.

VII. Dream Protection

When thinking about protection, what is the first thought that comes to mind? Did you think about a gun or other weapon? Did an alarm system keypad pop into your mind? Depending on what you wanted to keep safe, would determine what entered into your mind. We can go as far as thinking about a contraceptive device, which is protection as well.

People have the right to protect what belongs to them whether it is family or property. Systems are set up to ensure the safety of what is valuable. Consider your dream as falling under the umbrella of what you have the right to protect or to keep safe. To protect your dream is the ability to foresee what will come against it to plan a counterattack. Your goal is to see your dream come into manifestation therefore you must protect it as a parent does a child.

Remember, what you are chasing after is different and the level of protection you will need to safeguard your dream will be different as well. This is a set of principles to get you on the right track of knowing what to expect as to prevent being blindsided. Customize them accordingly.

The chapter Delete and Defeat Your Demons exposed a lot of things to be cautious of most of which were internal; things that may be a part of your character. This chapter digs into the things your dream will need to grow preventing extinction as well as enlightening you of the things to be aware of during the process of development.

During a word study, I decided to look up synonyms of the word *protection*. The first to show up due to the list being alphabetized was the word *ammunition*. After further looking through the list, it never listed *gun*. I pondered on this for a moment until it came to me. The weapon can be thought of as protection not realizing the gun is useless without the bullets unless you throw it at someone hitting them in the eye. Now I ask you what is your ammunition that can be launched to put a stop to or stun that which is coming against your life's goals? The following paragraphs are going to be filled with phrases, comments, and knowledge to help you surround your dream with the protection it needs in order to further strengthen it. These paragraphs are designed to provoke a thought process of security to protect what is rightfully yours.

DREAM INVESTMENT

In the financial world, ROI (Return On Investment) is very important to judge if something was a good investment or not. If the ROI is high then it was, but if the cost comes out to be greater, then it was not. How much are you willing to invest into your own dreams? Your investment is a part of the way you protect the goal. No one else should invest more into it than you do.

Usually when speaking of an investment, people tend to think monetary. Although you will get to the point that you have to invest money into your dream, there are other ways you need to invest which may not cost you one red cent. Trying to avoid an out of pocket expense will help you to creatively maintain growth while warding off stagnation. That statement alone lays out the fact there is no excuse for you to not make any progress.

One of the most important investments that will not cost you anything is time. It is your dream, your goal and you must be willing to invest the time into it. Time is money. The more time you spend on yourself could increase your value if it is appropriated into the right places. Your ROI will be effected by how productive you are with the time you have. When given time, a precious commodity that is very scarce, spend it wisely. There are only 24 hours within a day and with families, jobs and other responsibilities, this could be spent very fast.

To ensure that time is well spent will require you to do some planning. Delegating time is very important. If you happen to have a three hour window, please do not haphazardly use the time without setting clear cut boundaries for it. When you make a list allocating the task and the time to be spent on the particular task, you will be amazed at how much gets done. Here is a warning; try to keep tasks at a maximum of one hour spent in one sitting. The following example will bring enlightenment.

After everything is done and your regular responsibilities have been taken care of, you decide you have about four hours to work on your goal. Sit down to make a list of what you need to get done putting a time of one hour or less per task. When you know you only have fifty-nine more minutes left before the alarm goes off and you are to switch tasks, your mind can focus producing more from that small amount of time than if it had a large window of it. Even if the particular task you have chosen is large enough that you really need to work on it for two hours, after one hour switch tasks anyway for at least thirty minutes before scheduling another one hour session. When you try this, it will amaze you at how much you get done. Remember this is about spending time wisely.

There is a saying that states, "Job knowledge is job security." The whole point of this saying is to let people know the more they know about what they are doing the more secure it can be. This brings forth another investment that needs to be made to add to the protection of your dream and that is education. Education does not always have to come in the form of enrolling in a university but it is the increasing of your knowledge in the particular area that you are soon to be deemed an expert. A free source of education is the library which is full of resources in which some information about your particular goal is bound to be in the company of.

Outside of the library is yet another source of the internet, which has loads of information that has to be weeded through with caution. However, many great blogs, videos, and books can be found by simply typing in your interest. Search for workshops or online classes that may only contain a minimum fee. One of my favorites are master classes taught by individuals who are at the top of their game in their particular field. There is always someone online who does what you are trying to do and they do not mind sharing the information freely or for a fee. Remember you have to be your biggest investor but asking the right questions can save your wallet. You have to make sure you have done enough digging so you will know what question to ask and when.

A few years ago, I was going to happily share some information with some writers who came to me with publishing questions. I had only one request for them first; do some research on the publishing process. I gave them their assignment and then set an appointment for one week later. When the day came, the first question that came out of my mouth was, "What did you find out?" After blinking twice, both of them had the same answer; "I didn't have time." That is an insult to the person that is willing to spend time telling you everything. Then on the flipside, it lets that person know you are not serious about what you are seeking after.

So after getting that response from them both, I happily packed my stuff up and told them that I did not have time either. Remember, time is money. I did not have time to lay out the entire process from ground zero. However, I did have a few moments to fill in some blanks and answer some questions. In order for me to spend that amount of time with them, it would need to be in the format of a class or seminar in which I would have been getting paid for the time.

If you do not do a certain level of research, then you are not going to be able to formulate the correct questions that are going to get you the golden nuggets that you need to progress along. So invest in yourself first and then others will follow.

No Carbon Copies Welcomed

In your research, you are going to find a lot of people doing what you wish to do and it is going to look so appetizing that you may be tempted to follow someone else's plan with exact precision. Take this forewarning and do not do it. This warning was given briefly in the chapter Declare It. Now it is time for me to expound upon it in a way that you understand that resisting becoming a carbon copy is a means of protecting your dream.

However you choose to practice or motivate yourself, just remember that you do not watch the star of your dream to mimic what they are doing but you watch them to gain the motivation that you can achieve it also. After you have put months or maybe years into doing what you do, the worst thing ever is to realize that you have become a carbon copy or copycat of someone else whose dream is going to wind up somewhere differently than yours. Ouch!

Stay in your own lane. In other words, be yourself. There are many dreams that may have similarities but the dreamer has a different set of DNA, which means that there should always be something different about the purpose, structure, and destination of the dream. A popular fast food chain sells hamburgers but that does not mean that you cannot sell your burgers the way that you like them. If you want to mimic a particular establishment, buy franchise license. Otherwise, be unique. You will always have your own audience or customers that will buy what you are selling as long as they can see the difference.

The dangers of crossing over into someone else's lane is that you may trip up with someone that is in your blindside. Or even worse, you may get run completely over by someone that is in full speed ahead being themselves, running in their own lane. Then when you are sitting on the sidelines nursing your wounds, figure out why you wanted to change lanes. Sometimes we may notice that there was a slight twinge of jealousy because we have been doing something for a long time and the newcomer comes in making progress much faster with better results. If so, delete and defeat that demon immediately. A real dream chaser does not carry a spirit of jealousy. They understand their assignment to the point they know they only compete against opposition and other nonproductive versions of themselves.

Chasing after your individual dream is so that you can leave your unique fingerprint on it. When you are digging for knowledge, it is for the reasons of encouraging yourself that it can be done and to help in figuring out some things to possibly avoid. If it is copied, then it was done by you but you cannot be seen in it. You have so much to leave this world that duplicating what someone else does would be robbing others of the experience called YOU.

Imagine you have your dream home planned out in your head. You tell the architect exactly what you want with all the specifications as you have dreamt about them so many times. The kitchen is to be a specific size and open to the living room so family interactions will never be blocked by a wall. Then when you get ready to see the finished product, it is nothing like you told him to draw up and his only answer is, "I already had a blueprint that I use for everybody." Your would have been dream home is a cookie cutter home. No open concept to appease all the dinners cooked while watching the game with the rest of the family that you once envisioned. Sadly, you have paid the price to be like others.

It is not a rare event that people do this wondering why they do not feel the satiety they thought they would. Carbon copies are boring and they are not welcome by a world that is swiftly evolving. Consumers dictate inventors to not just think outside of the box but to crush it; their thirst is high for the newest and most different item. It is their means of being different even if just for a season until everyone else buys it too. So in order to be welcomed, you must be different. You must be you.

There are ways to take what someone else has done and immerge yourself into it. You have to be creative enough to find out how. It is inside of you and will be revealed once you embrace the difference and begin to brainstorm on how to meet your goal without excluding yourself.

DREAM KILLER VS DREAM MURDERER

You are excitedly working along on your dream when certain people begin to show up in your life. At first, they were welcomed; they are just friendly people. Then when you mention your goals or dreams, they seem to change. There is a level of aggravation within you that was not there before so you attribute it to staying up too late last night when in fact your alarm is blaring that there is an intruder. A killer is on the loose.

People that are doing something worthwhile typically have some type of opposition they need to protect themselves against. The first enemy you need to be aware of is a Dream Killer. By definition, a killer is someone that kills someone or something; one that is extremely difficult to deal with. If you are going to protect yourself against this type of person then you must know how to identify them.

The amazing thing about Dream Killers is that we all know them. Sometimes they are as close as a spouse, other family member, or your best friend. Yet the closest, most tragic, and deadliest Dream Killer is when it is you. Ouch! But we are going to assume that you are not on the list since you already learned how to delete and defeat your demons. However, what about other people who cause destruction to your dream in the most subtle way?

Chances are that some Dream Killers do not know they are. Some of them are just needy people who desire to consume large amounts of your attention but your dream got in the way. The way you recognize them is by their actions after certain statements that you make. "I can't talk any today because I'm working on a goal," and they blow your phone up all day with crisis after crisis and anything to get some of your time. They are competing with your dream for your attention. Intentional or not, they are a Dream Killer. Perhaps they are not consciously trying to destroy you or your dream whereas they are just being themselves. When that need for attention rises up, they can get it from anywhere like a serial killer because they are only feeding their desire. Believe it or not, if you do not lose your cool, this person is kind of easy to get rid of; give them an assignment that occupies their time. If you think that it is intentional, disassociate yourself from them. Since it is their toxic, overbearing traits that are distracting, be creative to come up with diversions for them.

Now what do you do if you have discovered someone more vicious has picked up your scent? This is a different level known as a Dream Murderer. These are those negative people that will attempt to speak a dagger into the heart of your dream at all cost. What makes them different? It is all in the definition.

Murder: *the crime of **deliberately** killing a person especially with **malice aforethought**.*

This type of person deliberately sought you out because they had something against you that they have been planning to attack you for quite some time. When you begin to go after a goal, that is the moment they strike hoping to release poisonous venom into the life of your dreams. The most remarkable yet unbelievable part about it all is that there is no justification for this attack. Plain and simple, they just don't like you.

Revisiting the story of Joseph, I'll attempt to explain the senseless actions of a Dream Murderer. When Joseph was young, he told his father the bad things his brothers did. Jacob already loved Joseph more and now he is telling on them. The brothers hid the hate they had for him. Then he had a dream and they hated him even more. After that, he had another dream. By now, they are consumed with hatred towards him. One day the opportunity presents itself for them to lash out on him. They see him coming from a distance and begin to plot to kill him making the statement, "Then we'll see what becomes of his dreams." Joseph gets striped of his beautiful coat that his father made for him and thrown into a pit before being sold instead of killed.

How does this relate to you? When you are dealing with envious people, any little thing can set them off. Let someone adore you more or brag one too many times about the great things you have done in their presence. Therefore, when you come up with something fabulous, you make them look bad in front of others because of their lack of doing. Chances are someone is endorsing you they may want the attention of. Although it is silly, but they hate you based on the actions of others who you have no control over. When they see you gaining ground they can see you from a mile away. They throw everything at you they can to make the dream die for the mere fact they want to be able to call you a failure to make themselves look better. Ultimately, they want to take your thunder or force you to stop standing out.

This is a dangerous person. If they cannot murder your dream they will do something equivalent; desecrate your character just to stop you from shining. Cain killed Abel because God was pleased with Abel's offering and not his. Joseph's brothers were willing to kill him because their father had more love for Joseph. In spite of how a Dream Murderer has the opportunity to just do better, they find it more rewarding to put a stop to you.

Warning: Do not be naïve in thinking this person is easily spotted; they sometimes come as harmlessly friendly like a wolf in sheep's clothing. Unless you are a mind reader, you never know what they are thinking and why. They have to be nice to get next to you to find out key pieces of information to be able to destroy what you hold dear. Remember they have to find a way to put out your spotlight and the only way to do it is to gain your confidence.

Revisit the chapter, Don't Tell It; Live It, to be reminded of why to be careful with your speech. So for now I will just stick to the specifics of a Dream Murderer. Importantly, it is best to know how to identify this type of person although in the beginning you will not but eventually they will slip up; you will see the tale sticking out or the wolf's tracks.

After getting the information they need, you will begin to see slight signs of them entering unnecessary competitions with you, ones you did not know you had signed up for. It is these very petty things that after being done numerous times will begin to wave a flag before you.

Then this competition becomes more cutthroat, very unscrupulous with bouts of manipulation. They are turning up the attacks which are becoming more vicious in nature. Once they have been exposed, they may seem relieved to not have to masquerade as an ally anymore. Remember, they have a desire or a damaged emotion that is driving them to shut you down. The way to prevent this from happening is to finish the one opposing you with their own weapon.

Jesus was on the cross with the enemy, a Dream Murderer thinking he had killed what Jesus was setting out to do because his body was dying. Nevertheless, when Jesus spoke the words, "It is finished," those words had the power to rob the Dream Murderer of any supposed victory he thought he had. Jesus used his death on the cross to capture the victory.

Unlike the Dream Killer, the Dream Murderer cannot just be disassociated from; there is a level of defeat that must take place to totally annihilate them. If it was the information they were after in the beginning then recount what you may have divulged to them or what they may have deciphered on their own. Take this information and set up blockers so they cannot use it against you. With you not being able to act like them, you must retain integrity which will ultimately seal the defeat. There is no defeat like reaching the goal this enemy desired to halt. Saying, "It is finished," slams the door.

One last caveat in this section will be to never discredit anyone from being the one who will come against you whether as a Dream Killer or Murderer. Both can be a hindrance to your dream but they do not have to be victorious. Joseph, once making it to the pinnacle of the dream, never treated his brothers with hate. When they come against you, take it as a sign that you are in the right place with something valuable. Recognize it and protect it.

Dream Motivator

Protect your dream at all cost. Even if the one who yielded the most destruction has the same fingerprints as yourself, buckle down and defeat the destructive version of yourself. A Dream Chaser has to do what a Dream Chaser has to do to make it to the finish line.

VIII. Decoding the Detours

One day while driving, I came to a section in which there was construction being done on the highway. With it being a small road that I was very familiar with, there were many other routes that could have been taken. From a point of impatience, detouring was my first thought. Gathering the different routes in my mind, mentally driving each one of them deciphering which would be the best to take. Doing this caused me to settle myself enough to wait; the feeling of the Pilot truck returning soon to lead us around construction overruled detouring.

As soon as the decision to stay was made, vehicles that were ahead of me began pulling out of line going the direction I had previously mapped out. My thoughts turned to question how long they had been waiting. However, something kept telling me to stick to this course. Then more cars detoured. I began to think that maybe the pilot truck was not coming. Yet, I stayed.

In the process of me staying, my cellphone rang with a business proposition I had been waiting on. After getting off the call an interesting revelation came that since I did not detour, something pertaining to my dream came to me. Then soon after, the pilot truck came.

Had a detour been made at this particular time, it would have cost something. It would have cost time, extra gas, and frustration from all the extra turns that would have had to be made. In the wait, a straight shot to the destination was provided. This is the same when it pertains to detouring with our dreams. However, there will be times in which a detour could be necessary as a means of protection. Knowing how to decode the detours will prove beneficial.

DEVIATION VS DIVERSION

What can be considered a detour with your dreams? It is very important to know this for the time when one is presented. A detour in dreams is something that is designed to get you off course or make you step aside from the initial plan. When the course which takes you outside of the goal is the one being travelled, then a detour has occurred. There are two ways to look at a detour; is it a deviation or a diversion?

One of my mental cues, a scripture, for this area is Proverbs 14:12. *"There is a way which seems right to man (Me), but the end thereof are the ways of death (Regret)."*

As you can tell, I have added my own amplifications to it which should be applied to mental cues in order for them to become personal. See yourself in what inspires you.

Here is a real scenario from my life to explain a deviation. I was at a point in which I had two books coming out and I was getting speaking engagements coming in from all over the place. That was great for those are areas that I dream of being in. Then here comes a business proposal to do sales in a completely different area. It was stated that I could use the experience gained from this new proposal to help me with my already existent writing and speaking career. Then it was further explained how this new venture could even help fund my current goals.

Well, looking at it from one angle it made a lot of sense, but when looking at it with my peripheral vision, I saw that it would become a deviation. What was going to make it a bad choice is that I would have to take valuable time away from doing the things I was already happily involved in to train, study, and do something that was in a completely different area in which I had zero passion for.

To deviate from something, by definition, is to stray especially from a standard, principle, or topic; to depart significantly from an established course. This is when the circumstance is causing a change taking the power from you, the controller. Yes. Things are going to come up all the time but do not relinquish the power over for it to begin to dictate the dream. You can make a choice. So choose wisely. Take the reins of your dream back into your hands before you not only deviate from the goal but you altogether abandon it.

A deviation can cause you to change your mind about what it is that you want to accomplish presenting alternatives which conflicts your mind so terribly until it kills your desire for the original goal. Be careful.

Although the words, deviation and diversion, are closely related the latter is different in a good way; they should not be equated with one another. Allow me to draw your attention to a movie where the characters attempt to get a particular person safely to a certain area. One brave person goes out as a diversion, drawing attention away from the others so they can arrive safely. In a nutshell, that is the definition of diversion; drawing attention away from the point of the principal operation—the dream.

Why would a diversion be needed when going after a goal? There are times in which you have drawn the attention of an enemy, such as the ones talked about in Dream Protection or you may have told the dream instead of living it. Now that you have the awareness of what is going on, you need to divert the attention away from the goal to protect it. This type of detour is necessary as it has a way shielding the dream from certain impending attacks.

Most goals should be multileveled. This is where it has branches stemming from the initial goal. Just like a natural tree, it does not kill the entire tree to lose one branch. In the following scenario a diversion will be explained in a way to bring some clarity.

Susie's ultimate dream is writing books and dispersing different items which are motivating to others. Her gift is writing which means writing in different areas is a possibility without having to put too much time or effort into it. One day she spills too much information about the next book and seminars she is working on causing opposition to arise. The diversion comes in when she begins talking about and doing poetry shows. While she is on the stage reciting poetry, it takes the attention away from the book and seminars which she is still working on and brings it onto the poetry which she loves as well. To lose that particular branch is not as painful since it is neither the tree nor the main goal.

Do you understand better how this particular type of detour works out in your favor? You are confusing those who want to put a stop to your goal. The funny thing about it is that when writers have writer's block the best thing to break it is to divert away from the work that is currently being worked on to do something else. When the motivation to return to the previous work comes, it is so powerful of how lost time is made up with the quality of the work which really means there was nothing lost. Be creative when this has to be applied to the particular goal you have.

Don't Abort

Earlier, I spoke briefly on how a deviation can quite possibly cause an abandonment to occur. This is something you want to be very leery of. What could be something that could arise in such a way as to have you prematurely cancel the dream chasing efforts before completion to remain in the realm of mediocrity? What could be so bad that it causes you to terminate going after the goal in its early stages before what could have been manifested can be seen? These are questions that need to be asked in advance to avoid aborting the dream because of problems and complications.

Problems are going to arise bringing stress to your efforts. However, you must find a way to go around the problem so that it will not cause you to make a permanent decision for a temporary situation. Develop a tough skin. Patience in the storm is going to be the key to the dream's survival. Looking back at the scenario involving Susie, if she would have quit, then the people she was assigned to reach would have never been motivated by her words. Your assignment is not completely about you.

Generally, accepting responsibility for the attack is the first response. "I'm under attack because I am doing something." So often we think that is the cause of the fiery darts that comes our way, but it is not altogether true. Some of the things we go through are because we are reaping something we sowed. Outside of that reason, what I want you to see is that the storm is about who you will connect with in the future. The storm is designed to get you off focus and to keep you from getting to your intended assignment.

A great storm arose when Jesus and the disciples were crossing over into an area where a man plagued by demons was living in the tombs. Had they turned around because of the temporary circumstance called bad weather, quite possibly this man would have never gotten his deliverance. It is not always about you.

Another yet more powerful example is when Jesus went onto the cross. Had he looked at the torture He was facing that would be followed by death and decided to abort the mission of getting onto the cross, quite possibly there would be no redemption for us today. It is not always about you.

The gifts you were given, ultimately are so God can get the glory out of your life. So do not abort the mission, walk away from the assignment because the battle gets rough. Someone needs you to stay the course even if that person was the nonproductive version of yourself. Don't quit.

Develop Discipline

Discipline is a dirty word when you lack it. It just throws your mental faculties into a state of shock to transition from flying by the seat of your pants to following a set of rules which require self-control. When on the road to your purpose, discipline must have the loudest voice. Discipline tells you to continue even past quitting time; stay the course when no one is cheering you on; not to abort for the benefit of others. This structure is detrimental to the efforts of wanting to throw in the towel.

The key thing about discipline, in the form being discussed, cannot be given; it is acquired by change of behavior. To change inward attributes can be much harder to do than if changing others. This needs to be developed as time progresses. This is the period of time in which you learn all about your weaknesses and strengths.

The reason this behavior is so important when it comes to decoding the detours is for the very reason that you do not inflict your own thoughts upon the decision making processes of the dream. That will allow you to remain the way you are. You must remember it was something or a lack of it in the past being the reason you did not accomplish the goal last time. Now is not the time to stick with familiar as it is deadly to success.

Hiccups of Life

Hiccups are signs there is something else that wants to be added to your life. That something is going to make everything else seem right but only if you do it. It is an incredible thing to find the missing piece to the puzzle. Clarity seems to come to you like a cool breeze on a hot sweat provoking day. You feel relieved. That is why you have to recognize what it is that you have to do to fulfill your destiny. What is that one thing or your next thing that is the cool breeze to your life? What is the next chapter of your life that simply cannot be left out of your own book? It is very important to find out what it is and do it.

Look at it this way. One day many years from now, you take a long hard look at your life. You see these hiccups in your life wondering what the meaning of it was. Then you realize that those are the spots in which you could have added something significant into your life. It could have been something small like telling the man that you passed on the street who had a depressed countenance to, "Have a great day." Those four words could have been the start to your motivational speaking career in which you would have felt as if you were fulfilling your life's purpose.

Or what if your hiccup was when you ignored those words that kept clamoring your brain to be put down on paper. You could have ignored the script that would have landed you to being a famous and most sought after screenwriter.

Or what if the day that you thought that guy who approached you was just like all the rest of them but in actuality you waving him off was the hiccup that kept you from being happily married? Now that you never married, you look back on it from a place that wanting to marry has been suffocated, to see that you could have been happily married to the one that was never given a chance.

Whatever your hiccup could be, by you starting to read right now is going to be equivalent to holding your breath, drinking some water or getting someone to scare the crap out of you so that you don't allow that hiccup to interrupt the rest of your life. You never want to have should've, would've, could've moments to look back on. These are the times that you regret because you know not only should you have done it but you see that if you would have done something that you know that you could have done you would be in a better place; a place called Freedom. This level of regret is devastating. I have up close and personal firsthand knowledge of this type of devastation. Trust me. You don't want to visit this place.

However, for those of you that have already become acquainted with it, turn it around to use that tormenting feeling which just crawled across your brain to be the fuel that you need to never allow it to happen again. This is the moment that you realize that you have to do it even if it is to escape regret. The fewer hiccups that you have the better off you will feel. In the long run, you will come to a place that you will be Free.

After my mother passed away, I realized that instead of just doing poetry I was supposed to be a writer of various works. She always saw it and said it to me. I always felt its tugging but took so many detours that deviated me away from my true purpose in life. But after she passed I was filled with the regret of not showing her that what she knew all along was correct. I would like for you to know who you are and live your life powerfully. Walk the path you were given and make it fabulous.

Dream Motivator

Live life without actions that causes regrets.

—*Kimberley M. Byrd*

IX. Develop Positive Connections

"What I know now is that we're all interconnected and that's a really beautiful thing. We have links to everyone else in our lives and in the world. Different people have different reasons. You can't judge, but you can celebrate that there are connections everywhere."—Jane Seymour

As humans, connections are a part of our survival. Should we fail to connect, we will fail to exist. It is most important we make the right connections throughout life and even more important when trying to accomplish a life's goal.

Complete independence upon self does not really exist. Think back to the earlier chapter, Daily Bread, where it was written that others might know more. When forming positive connections, being humble must sometimes take precedence over the goal in order to reach the goal. If you fail to connect with the correct person due to prideful reasons, there could be a setback. What if Joseph failed to let go of bitterness because he knew he was right? Very possibly, he would have never connected with Pharaoh causing the dream to happen. Whom you connect with or whom you reject is very detrimental to your dream chasing efforts. Rejecting someone you were supposed to connect with could land you in a place so negatively charged it kills any hope of reaching the finish line.

Just like the wellbeing of our children being important enough to us that we sacrifice for them, so must it be for the dream. Have the mindset that there are others out there who could be an insurmountable help to your progress. Not everyone is against you.

Finding a Mentor

Who could be the person who has enough influence to convince you to succeed? Who would be able to cater to the needs of your aspirations in such a way it positively drives you? This person will be one that has motivation and cold truth both dripping from their lips. They are mentors and even the most influential people who have ever walked the earth have had one.

Mentors are looked up to for the advice or guidance they give. This advice should be in the realm of qualitative over quantitative; it's not how much is given, but how impactful it is. People who have the power to condense into one sentence what it may take someone else paragraphs really knows what they are talking about. They have been surrounded by the information they present for quite some time. If what they have spoken is received, then over time it will continually unfold giving directions even when the mentor is not presently speaking.

Has a quote or comment ever latched itself to your heart in a way forgetting about it was nearly impossible? It had such a way of holding your thoughts captive until its true meaning is conceived. Things like these can enhance your life if applied properly.

However, this is not what to expect from the beginning as the mentor must perceive the mindset of the mentee or protégé. On the opposite side, the student must also decide whether to accept this person as a confidant. If that trust is never constructed properly, then the one learning will neither release nor receive to the highest benefit. There will be something missing as the mentor cannot give the appropriate advice if parts of the puzzle is missing due to the fear to divulge information being prevalent. The mentor must be someone entrusted to contain key information about your strengths as well as your weaknesses. This is not the time to cover up in a way to paint a perfect picture about yourself. Choose someone who you can open up to. Choose carefully.

Not everyone can be your mentor. It can be easy to think that someone who has succeeded in the area you are entering could be the perfect mentor. This is not always true. Some people are wonderful at doing but they are not equal in teaching. They will, not intentionally, steer you way off course simply because they do not have the ability to instruct others. Do not discredit the person who has accomplishments in a different set of goals; if they know how to instruct then they will know how to cater the information so it will be beneficial to you in what you are doing.

When you look to make that connection be wise and discerning because you are embarking on something very dear to you. Depending on what you are trying to do, you may not need a personal mentor at all but can suffice with being in a group of people where you all share a common interest. There are ways to seek them out and see which one fits you.

Virus Protection Software

Everywhere you look, different companies are offering their version of virus protection. Some of them are promising one thing and others another. Then there are the giants in it, which are the most sought out, the most trusted name in the business of the virus protection software. The cost is greater, but there is so much more that comes with the package plus an assuredness of their product that they even guarantee it. A team stands behind the product to offer support to the purchaser should they need it. In addition, of the same software, levels of protection are offered based on what is being protected; email, internet search, or the overall computer system.

With that being said, do you have virus protection software? Not on your computer but is there someone who acts as this kind of software when it comes to your motivational level when you are doing something significant. Your mind is like a computer and if you allow deadly things to infect it, then it will kill your dream chaser efforts. Of course, your mind, your internal software should be set to knock these attempts down but there are some which comes so covertly until the recognition of it being an attack is not detected. Way down the line, you realized what has happened. Now, the time of digging yourself out of the hole starts which some people lose all desire to do this work. You have suffered under the hands of a malicious virus.

Discouragement is a mighty virus with its subtle actions designed to make you give up. This particular virus is planted in different forms until the one that works is found. Doubt, fear tactics, false concern and numerous ways of planting a virus have already been discussed throughout this book. However, there are people who are gifted in the area of keeping others motivated. The moment something negative fires your way, they have the ability to put a force field around your mind in such a way the attack bounces off. What does this person look like?

My nephew Benjamin discussed some of his goals in life with me. I latched onto believing with him that he was going to achieve these very things. Every month or so, without warning, my thoughts turn to him and what he is doing. It is almost as if I feel the need to encourage him and to ask specific questions. This process I call checking his temperature. The purpose behind checking his temperature every so often is to make sure he is still on the hot track towards his dreams. In addition to, its other reason is to counterattack anything that has come against him. Has someone planted a phrase to make him doubt he can do it? Did someone use fear tactics to scare him away from trying? Or, did someone slide up next to him using false concern to negatively encourage him that the dream is too much for him and it is ok to quit. No! It's not.

Even though there are the boundaries of states between us, this encouragement is sent through a text message, phone call, or whatever. As long as the message is given, that is all that counts. It does not matter if we can see each other on a daily basis. It does not matter about being able to have a lengthy conversation about what he is doing. It does not matter about getting details of his efforts. The only thing that matters is he receives the encouragement to keep going.

In your own life, there may be a person that comes similar to this. Sometimes it may even look as if they are prying into your life. Remember back to the beginning of the chapter to learn how to decipher if they are someone you need to connect with or reject. It would be a great tragedy if you rejected your virus protection; the one sent to motivate you.

If you have found that you have one of these people in your life already, rejoice because you are blessed. Too often people are so focused on themselves that they do not think it rewarding to encourage someone else. What people do not realize is that the one who motivates you gets hit just as an intercessor does because they have stepped in between the person and the desire to quit. You need to pray for your virus protection.

One last thing on this topic, never feel grieved when they are not around you all the time or anymore. Motivation can be given from a distance. Also, if you have noticed they are not there for you anymore, that is only because their part of the assignment is over. Some people take this separation hard because they see it as personal. If you can skip this season of feeling a loss, then you can use the momentum of what they have given you to the fullest capacity. This last comment is purposefully postscript to the two; the mentor and the virus protection. They do not have to be nor will they always be the same person. The mentor gives you the know how while the virus protection keeps you believing that you can do it somehow.

As already mentioned in this section, it is great to have external protection added to your internal one. In the movie X-Men: Days of Future Past, Professor X encouraged the younger version of himself to do something great in his time so that it would positively affect the future. In the present time, Professor X was under attack and death was right outside the door. Therefore, he needed his younger version to know that he could make the right decision so that it would alter his future. Watch the movie. You'll understand what I am talking about.

However, the point is this. You need to be able to connect with yourself in a way that you can gauge your own temperature. How did what others specified your limits are touch you? Did their comments sway you in a negative way? Did someone, out of false concern, almost cause you to quit? The more you ask yourself these questions, the more equipped you will be at the onset of an attack.

Regardless of who cheers or does not cheer for you, there has to be something on the inside that will not give in. Remember that when God is on your side, then you are basically set for the long haul. You are closer to your dream. You got this!

Unequally Yoked?

Synergy. The increased effectiveness that results when two or more people or businesses work together. Based upon its definition, synergy is when you and another work together towards your goal it becomes more advantageous had you went it alone. Two minds have the ability to pull the best from each other by taking turns to expound upon the same idea. When this is completed, the basic idea from the beginning has become something multileveled.

There are many people out there who need a brainstorming partner they can trust to bounce ideas off. Notice the key word is trust. Can you trust this person to not run off with your fabulous idea? But are the people who have already earned your trust goal oriented enough to push you towards your dream? If so, why have you not found achievement in that area?

When it comes down to rolling up sleeves to put the work in to reach the goal, not everyone understands the level of motivation it will take to make it happen. If they lack this knowledge, they will be lost when it is time to give you the right nugget of encouragement you need to make it to the next step. They just do not know. They may be the individual who will talk to you about dreams all day long but never put anything to paper nor complete the work. They get excited about brainstorming but never progress past this point. Therefore, you have wasted time because you are not connected with the correct one.

In going after something, especially something you have never done, it is very important to be equally yoked, joined together. Compatibility is going to be to your advantage. Find someone that has a 'Go get it' or 'Get it done' attitude. They do not even have to be going after what you are going after but they may have the knowledge of how to get it done. Think back to my dad asking his dad for advice. There are people out there with medical degrees yet they do not practice medicine; they teach others instead. Not everyone can just *be* but they must lead or push others to *become*.

This next statement is going to be shocking to you, but hear me out before discrediting me. Sometimes that Dream Killer (NOT the Dream Murderer) could be the one you need to connect with. What? Take the information I told you about Dream Killers and look over it very carefully. I said they mostly come against your dream because they have to compete with it for your time and the way to get rid of them is to give them an assignment. If they can be trusted, why not make that assignment something on your to-do list. A Dream Killer could be a positive connection once you have redirected their energy. Have them focused on completing a task for you that will help in your advancement versus them being a distraction. After all, they wanted your attention and knowing that they are helping you will be a big booster for them.

Warning! I am not advising you to misuse anyone. People have feelings and it will be abusive for you to have these people slaving and doing more work than you. That is never the right way to do things. Reward them for what they do. Pay them for their work. But first and more importantly, make an offer to them to see if that is something they would be willing to do. Taking advantage of someone will always backfire on you. You will reap what you sow.

However, there will be people that you are going to meet along your journey. Do not be wounded when some fall off. It is ok since they were only there to get you to the level where they fell away. No one person has all the pieces that you are going to need. Keep an open mind and be ready to size up the reason the next person comes into your life.

DOORS OF OPPORTUNITY

One day I was sitting outside a grocery store. I observed a little boy on the inside attempting to get the automatic doors to open. He jumped. No affect. He waved. Still nothing. Then as a man approached the door from the outside, the little boy got what he wanted. The doors came open sending in enough wind to make his hair ruffle. After a short period with this little boy still standing in front of these doors, they closed.

Then he went back to his previous actions to no avail once again. After a little while longer, a girl who was shorter than he was started walking from the register towards the door. He did not see her as she was coming up behind him. When the doors opened, he thought what he had done worked this time. His face lit up like a Christmas tree. Even though this little girl was standing beside him now, it still had not registered that he had not caused the door to open. I dare not go tell him the truth unless I was just in the mood to be mean to a kid.

I learned a lesson from these two little ones that would one day, possibly very soon, be at the stature to have the door open without all the effort. I learned that you can try your hardest to get the door to open but what counts sometimes is getting into the right position; making the right connections. When you are walking in the right direction, the doors begin to fly open when you get to them. They will not open until you get there.

There are going to be people, connections who are going to be waiting on you to show up. God will have them in place to provide just what you need when you need it. The door will automatically open for you. As long as you are moving, you can make progress.

Here Joseph's story is going to make a lot of sense. He may have been going through a horrific time being displaced from his family with the majority of them being the ones responsible for it.

He had to make an internal decision that would prove to be detrimental to his success; keep moving in spite of.

There are going to be people that come along who will damage our tendency to trust. Do not allow them to make you miss your big opportunity. Keep moving anyhow and anyway you can. There are certain wounds that are necessary to make us adamant enough to decide to finish. When hit the right way by the right one, a certain level of insistence hits us making us unyielding to any more opposition. The hurt was a help to you as long as you do not dwell upon it making it a hindrance.

Joseph made a decision in slavery at Potiphar's house to not let his brothers' actions counterattack what God was doing. The door opened. He made a decision in prison that being falsely accused could not stop him. This door opened. Another decision made when he thought the cupbearer, whom he helped, had forgot all about him. Finally, the door to the palace opened. He was at his last test and had to perform optimally to get through this last one. With confidence, he entered. He was doing what he was good at, what he was purposed to do.

In dream chasing, realize that there are different types of doors just as there are in the natural. Banks have vaulted doors that open at a particular time. It may not be your time to walk through that particular door. Patiently, without injury or insult, wait. If a baby is born too soon then the risk of death is greater. The same thing is true with your baby, the dream that may be too premature to go to certain levels at its current stage of infancy, but when the time is right, nothing can stop the dream from advancing.

Then there are locked doors in which you need the right key to unlock. What do you offer that can make that door become unlocked? Have you asked the right questions? Multilevel thinkers, people who think on various levels of the dream, know how to ask the right questions to get them into the right position. It takes education in your area to do this. The more you know, the more you can formulate the proper question.

For instance, you are trying to get out of debt and one day you have a random elevator ride with a known self-made millionaire who once was in debt up to their eyeballs. Now, having only the time to ask one question, I would desperately hope your question would not be, "Hey, where did you get those shoes?" If that is not an icebreaker, which in an elevator you do not have time for, then you have failed.

The correct question will provoke an answer that will save you the time or any other precious commodity you would have spent trying to figure it out on your own. Knowing what questions to ask correlates with you knowing quite a bit about what you are doing. If the door represents the opportunity so does the answer to the right question equate to the key for the locked door. Open Sesame.

Next, let's look at the story about the little boy who was standing before an automatic door. These types of doors sense a presence that causes them to open but they only remain open for an appointed amount of time. You arrive at the time and are able to walk in. Great! That means you are right on schedule opening you up to different things that keep progress occurring.

However, with these same doors, when it is after business hours, they will not open regardless of the angle of approach, the stature of the one approaching, or the sensing of a presence. If they are forced open, it is breaking and entering, which is illegal. This is just how they are programmed. The door is locked. There are times in which a locked or a slammed shut door is a blessing. You should not walk through every door you come to anyway. Judge the door; judge the connection.

There may have been certain things you wanted in life, praying enough to call down fire from Heaven, yet nothing moved. You sense that denial is absolute and not delayed. Why? God gives you the desires of your heart, right? With limited sight,

DEVELOP POSITIVE CONNECTIONS

a closure is for the purpose of protection. If He cuts a connection, closes a door, be grateful, not wounded. Business hours are over for that particular connection.

Finally, revolving doors which are still doors but they go around in circles. That does not sound like something you want to do when going after anything in life. Seems as a waste of time to go around and around but this is not a carousel. This is a door. With this type of door, it takes effort to get them to move. They do not just open but they revolve around to you. You have to make them turn to open up to the right possibility. You have to push and walk. When inside of a revolving door, you are walking inside of your opportunity. Where you get off is up to you. Although if you walk inside of opportunity or take too long to make a decision, you will wind up back where you started; outside on the street. Then you will have to wait for the chance to get back inside of your opportunity.

It takes making the right connections to get here. And there are going to be times in which you totally miss it. While you are waiting for opportunity to come back around, work on your skill; fine-tune some things that are not up to par. Reconsider if there is yet something else that needs deletion. Whatever made you miss the opportunity, get rid of it. If you procrastinated, get rid of it. If you were shy, revolve into boldness. In this time of waiting, become a better you. When you learn to use every opportunity, good or bad, for the advancement of your dream then you will soon be at the finish line. While you are outside on the street, look up to see all the floors of opportunities waiting for you to show up. Use being outside of your opportunity as a means of motivation revving your engine excitedly anticipating the next chance.

Very importantly, I repeat an earlier point by saying that you should not walk through every door. Everything that looks good may not always be in the long run. Sometimes you have to miss an opportunity, break a connection to make a better one. The multilevel thinker would figure this out when it is presented.

Look back at the goal. Carefully weigh the options when presented. Keep your eyes open for all kinds of possibilities, do your homework, form your questions before you need to ask them, and never ever quit.

Door after door, Joseph had to decide to walk through whichever one it was. By continuously moving in spite of, he transitioned from dreaming to interpreting and finally to living his dream.

Dream Motivator

There are some connections you will make which will seem to never get off the ground. However, there are those developments which are growing gradually into something elaborate. Just as a seed looks dead when it is dormant, the same is true for some experiences you will have. But when they begin to sprout…

X. Die Empty

When you have reached the finish line of life and you are making the decision of what to leave as an inheritance, what would it be? What is your most valuable possession? If your answer was not the dreams and gifts that have been downloaded into you, then you need to read this entire book again.

I once heard that the graveyard was the wealthiest place on earth. That statement was so very shocking until the meaning was expounded upon. So many people have died with dreams, inventions, businesses, and powerful gifts within themselves instead of going for it. They have chosen to take those valuable items with them to their final resting place instead of leaving them to a world that would have certainly appreciated the conveniences their gifts and knowledge would have offered. They left us, the survivors, to die by not releasing the cure; left us wanting to be revolutionized by not sharing the innovation. With themselves, they buried their brainchild. For whatever reason, they refused to die empty.

After reading this book, if you do not die empty that simply and straightforward means you are a coward. I know that hurt but this is my last attempt at jolting you to achieve the greatness that is on the inside of you. Dying empty is just saying you were audacious enough to pour out everything that was inside of you leaving it as an inheritance to the world. You did not ignore the tugging of your gift that wanted to live outside of you. The dream wanted to soar freely. Dying empty is the way you acknowledge this. You did what it took to gather the guts to become uncommonly extraordinary. Living a life of mediocrity was triumphantly cancelled. Being a Dream Chaser has afforded you the opportunity to do and be what you once thought to be just a dream.

Dream chasing, as you may have figured out, is a lot more complex than you thought. Yet its complexities are only there so that you find a point of simplicity. After you have built the necessary muscles, endurance, don't quit mentality, and have been suited up for the battle, it will not be long before you see the thing that you were most passionate about. That is a special day in which you will be able to exhale victory. The battle got hot in some spots but it was worth it. You almost gave up sometimes but you did not resulting in a self-satisfaction you have never felt before. Some things almost made you lose your will to dream but you defeated the negative desire.

When you are that great wife, reaching the point in which you fulfill the part of the vows that says until death does its part. You spent a lifetime of happiness by his side and not one day did he miss telling you how great you are. On your last day, you will know that you not only chased the dream but you lived it.

Every time you look out the window of that nice house with the white picket fence to check on the kids, you will know that the penny-pinching days were worth it all to venture from renting to owning.

With every person that you teach how to get out of debt, you will be rewarded for the times in which you could not go on the spur of the moment shopping spree. You chose to do something that would be more gratifying in the end. You are debt free and equipped with the knowledge of how to stay that way.

When you see the flashing of the cameras, while you stand on the red carpet, you will know that you have arrived.

While flipping the pages of the newspaper, you see your book as number one on the bestsellers list. Your heart flutters since you know that you made it despite the times you almost quit.

Whatever the dream, your moment will come when you turn the key to the door that was once locked. Your moment comes often since you went from dreaming to dream chasing. Now every single day you not only dream but you live the dream. You ran the race through blood, sweat, and tears. The tape has been broken across your chest. Hands are in the air. You have won.

Welcome to the Winner's Circle! You definitely belong here.

MULTIPLY

Thought this was over didn't you? Yes. It is true the bulk of the information has been given, but this is what you do after finishing; you must multiply. If you are to be deemed completely successful, there must be a certain level of multiplicity seen. All that work for one harvest would be tragic. Now that you have the field cultivated or the path worn, why not duplicate what you have already done.

Whatever you had to go through, you will find that one day, simply, it was worth it all. You have accomplished a great feat. Now that you have accomplished one thing, you are equipped with the ability to do it again. There is more inside of you and now that you have started you might as well do it to the fullest. Keep delivering your inheritance to the world while you are still here so that you can be appreciated now. One day you will be held accountable for what you did or did not do with what you were given. As long as you are emptying yourself, your slate will be clean.

When new ideas are presented to your heart, accomplish them. In the season in which nothing is coming to you, there is another way to keep multiplying; show others. By showing others what you have learned is another way to communicate your growth in knowledge. You will then pull someone else out of the grave alive with his or her gifts. Give them some helpful nuggets you acquired along the way that could save them some time when they start their journey. Teach them to die empty.

Things you learn from personal experience are items you need to remember. More than likely you will acquire the knowledge that it takes as much if not more energy to finish as it does to start. There has to be a decision made and that is to decide to finish and finish well. Here is where you will have to dig your heels in and constantly remind yourself it is not quitting time.

When I think about this, I am reminded of a cartoon illustration I saw on the internet. There is a man digging a tunnel looking for diamonds. At the point he quit, the diamonds were one more strike away from being exposed to him. So I say to you, don't quit digging. Go for it with everything you have. Don't be afraid to guide others because what you make happen for others, God will make happen for you. Besides, Dream Chasers do not carry a spirit of jealousy because of all the excellence on the inside does not leave room for anything else.

Do it to the fullest. Dream It. Do It. Repeat! Dream like God is cheering for you; and He is indeed.

Dream Motivator

Be brave enough to rob the grave.

Final Words

On December 18, 2011, I spoke a message titled, "*I'm Not Going to Be Here Much Longer.*" Within that message, I was making certain declarations about my life, which was not going the way that I would have liked for it to. I was making the statement more so to myself than to anyone else that I have to leave stagnation in order to get to that place that I longed to be. My desire was to go up and to leave the comfort of mediocrity.

After making the statement, with every intention within my heart that it was true this time, my life took a turn for the absolute worse. The battle that I had been struggling with against Insomnia had increased—suddenly. Making that type of declaration had gotten me deeper into trouble but…

There are times in which the very moment that we decide that we are done with certain negative aspects of our lives that the fight gets harder. Why is that you might ask? It is for the simple reason that you are not the only one that got comfortable with you being around. Those negative conditions love your presence. You give them life. Now that you have decided to do better, it threatens to kill their existence. Also, it is not the fact that you said that you were going to do better that got you into hot water, it is the fact that you actually believe it this time. There were many other times that you may have firmly stated that you were not going to be in certain situations much longer but it was just words until it activated into your heart. Once inside your heart it ignited the passion, which changed your DNA. You are no longer that person that just wanted to do; now you are doing.

Look at it from the natural. Have you ever been in a relationship that you wanted to leave for whatever reason? Maybe your boyfriend had become abusive or perhaps your girlfriend was not the same woman that you fell in love with. You may say to others or to them that you are going to leave them yet no one believes you until the look in your eyes change. The saying that your eyes are the gateway to your soul is very true. When that look changes, then people believe what you are saying causing a challenge to arise. The person may beg you to stay with promises of doing better this time; they are no longer going to hit you; they can become that woman that you first met. Promise after promise is made but since you have said, "It is over," within your heart, nothing can change your mind. You are freeing yourself from captivity.

So that scenario can be used to explain why some of our negative attributes clinch down harder on us when we strive to do better. Procrastination calls out even louder to us as soon as we stop saying "I'll do it later," and start doing it now. Tardiness attempts to trip us up when we begin to hold punctuality close to our hearts. Then think about the biggest adversary to you accomplishing your dream. Does it call your entire name out with sweet empty promises once you decide that you are going to chase after the dream or desire that you hold dear on the inside?

Now that leads me back to the earlier statement that I was making about how my suffering from Insomnia increased traumatically the very moment that I wanted to go after my dream. Everything in my heart said, "I'm going to do it this time." Failure was not an option neither did it even come close to bothering me this time. Since I had not been chasing after my dream of writing, I was tormented to the point that I thought that I was going crazy. Therefore, I made up in my mind that it was now or never. The declaration hit the atmosphere and I went from suffering from bouts of Insomnia 2-3 times per year to suffering from Insomnia nonstop for all of 2012.

With many nights of only getting 2 or 3 hours of *interrupted* sleep, I was not going to physically make it. There were times that I thought that maybe my statement of not being here much longer was misinterpreted. Yet, there was something on the inside, a fight that was swelling up that would not allow me to settle for this. Now is the time resonated within my mind so much that sleep or the lack of it became a challenge I was determined to pass.

Nevertheless, two of my dreams happened; I pushed out another novel and I became a wife. Had I listened to the, "This is too hard," or "Just quit and do it later when the time is right," I would have never been able to write this book about how to not only chase after your dreams but to see dream manifestation. The 10 Commandments for Dream Chasers was downloaded within me as a sermon but the more I held onto it, the more it became a force that was going to be sent out to accomplish another one of my dreams—Motivate people. This is my way of multiplying.

Within the pages of this book, I hope you found the motivation needed for you to accomplish that dream that is on the inside of you. What you dream is up to you. I have just provided the motivation to push your dream. I will see you at the finish line.

ACKNOWLEDGEMENTS

First, I would like to thank and acknowledge the Almighty God, who's love has never failed me despite the times I've minimized what He's given me.

Thank you, LeCurtis for getting on board with the dreams and visions God has placed inside of me. Keep the prayers coming. I appreciate and need them. I've learned a lot being married to you.

Pastor James McClure, thank you for hearing from God and telling me just what I needed to hear to confirm what I asked. I think God gave you a special kind of glasses to see the need of the congregation you pastor.

To my awesome prayer partners, Diane McClure, Sandra Ikner, Mareta Tofaeono, and Cornelia Davis, thank you ladies for touching and agreeing with me before a God who hears His people. In addition, Cornelia, I am forever grateful you got me back onto the boat. Girl, it's full speed ahead.

A great big thank you to all my family and friends. Thank you for being supportive and loving.

Cornerstone of Life Y.A.Y.A.s, you are an awesome bunch of young people who I am very proud to know. I know you are going to become some fantabulous game changers and dream chasers one day soon.

And I can't leave out my little Gabby, my would've been daughter if her mother would have signed the papers. LOL. Gabby you are headstrong, very determined, and you think you can do anything. Those are the characteristics of a true dream chaser wrapped in a six-year old's body. Take the world by storm. I'll motivate you to do so. (wink)

Finally, I would be remised if I didn't thank you, the readers. I feel commissioned to write to empower you.

 **Kimberley M. Byrd** is a native of Alabama where she happily lives with her husband LeCurtis.

Her most favorite thing to do outside of smiling and writing is to motivate others. *Ten Commandments for Dream Chasers: Dream Like God is Cheering for You* is her first non-fiction. Developing the M.O.M. (Minister of Motivation) brand is her passion in which she breathes out uplifting statements via different channels mostly with a minute of motivation, sixty seconds of life changing videos.

Outside of being a motivator, Kimberley is the author of two novels; Forbidden Fruit and Son of the Forgiven. Her first love of poetry is always operational within her as she has penned well over 100 poems. In addition, she is a playwright who has brought to the stage *Daddy, I Need You* with *Under New Management* following close behind.

Kimberley serves as Youth Director at the Cornerstone of Life Church where she believes that all people have a purpose but sometimes needs guidance towards it.

Other Titles

The Dream Motivator: 30-Day Dream Chaser Journal

Forbidden Fruit (Book 1)

Son of the Forgiven (Book 2)

Social Media

Website: *www.WriteOnKim.com*

E-mail: *PageTurner@WriteOnKim.com*

Facebook: *Facebook.com/writeonkim*

Twitter: *@WriteOnKim*

www.ingramcontent.com/pod-product-compliance
Lightning Source LLC
LaVergne TN
LVHW051526070426
835507LV00023B/3319